WRITING
SMART

3rd Edition

The Staff of The Princeton Review

PrincetonReview.com

Penguin
Random
House

The Princeton Review
110 East 42nd St., 7th Floor
New York, NY 10017
Email: editorialsupport@review.com

Published in the United States by Penguin
Random House LLC, New York, and in Canada
by Random House of Canada, a division of
Penguin Random House Ltd., Toronto.

Some of the content in *Writing Smart, 3rd
Edition* has previously appeared in *Grammar
Smart, 4th Edition*, published as a trade paper-
back by Penguin Random House LLC in 2017.

Terms of Service: The Princeton Review
Online Companion Tools ("Student Tools") for
retail books are available for only the two most
recent editions of that book. Student Tools
may be activated only once per eligible book
purchased for a total of 24 months of access.
Activation of Student Tools more than once
per book is in direct violation of these Terms
of Service and may result in discontinuation
of access to Student Tools Services.

ISBN: 978-0-525-56758-5
eBook ISBN: 978-0-525-56771-4
ISSN: 2576-0688

The Princeton Review is not affiliated with
Princeton University.

Editor: Colleen Day
Production Editor: Liz Dacey
Production Artist: Deborah A. Weber
Content Contributor: Christine Lindwall

10 9 8 7 6 5 4 3 2 1

3rd Edition

Editorial

Rob Franek, Editor-in-Chief
Mary Beth Garrick, Executive Director of Production
Craig Patches, Production Design Manager
Selena Coppock, Managing Editor
Meave Shelton, Senior Editor
Colleen Day, Editor
Sarah Litt, Editor
Aaron Riccio, Editor
Orion McBean, Associate Editor

Penguin Random House Publishing Team

Tom Russell, VP, Publisher
Alison Stoltzfus, Publishing Director
Amanda Yee, Associate Managing Editor
Ellen Reed, Production Manager
Suzanne Lee, Designer

Acknowledgments

The Princeton Review would like to extend special thanks to Christine Lindwall for her valuable contributions to the third edition of this book. We are, as always, greatly appreciative of Debbie Weber and Liz Dacey for their time and attention to each page.

Contents

Get More (Free) Content

1 Go to **PrincetonReview.com/cracking**

2 Enter the following ISBN for your book: 9780525567585

3 Answer a few simple questions to set up an exclusive Princet[o] Review account. (If you already have one, you can just log in.[)]

4 Click the "Account Home" button, also found under "My Acco[unt] from the top toolbar. You're all set to access your bonus cont[ent]

Need to report a potential **content** issue?

Contact
EditorialSupport@review.com.
Include:

- full title of the book
- ISBN number
- page number

Need to report a **technical** issue?

Contact
TPRStudentTech@review.com
and provide:

- your full name
- email address used to regis[ter] the book
- full book title and ISBN
- computer OS (Mac/PC) an[d] browser (Firefox, Safari, etc[.])

nce you've registered, you can...

ownload a printable glossary of need-to-know grammar terms

et valuable advice about the college application process, cluding tips for writing a great essay and where to apply for nancial aid

you're still choosing between colleges, use our searchable nkings of *The Best 384 Colleges* to find out more information out your dream school.

neck to see if there have been any corrections or updates to this dition

fline Resources

ading Smart

ammar Smart

ord Smart

ore Word Smart

Introduction

"The difference between the almost right word
and the right word is...the difference between the
lightning bug and the lightning."

—Mark Twain

Why Are Writing Skills So Important?

The written word is a powerful tool. It can tell a story, inform, persuade, evoke emotion, and more—often more effectively than can be done verbally. The ability to write properly, effectively, and in a compelling manner can vastly improve your chances for success in almost any endeavor. People often form strong opinions about you based on your facility with the written word.

Unfortunately, however, the widespread use of modern technology has created the false impression that writing skills don't matter much anymore. After all, when texting and email allow for nearly instantaneous written communication, how can we hold such casual exchanges to any meaningful standard? Moreover, in the age of spellcheck and autocorrect, who really needs knowledge that our phones, tablets, and computers can store and apply for us? The truth is that we all do. Technology cannot compensate for poor writing skills. The inability to express yourself clearly creates a negative impression—even in the 21st century.

In some ways, writing standards are as stringent as ever. For example, standardized tests like the SAT and various AP Exams are moving toward an emphasis on writing skills. The SAT now has a Writing and Language section as well as an optional essay, while several AP Exams have been redesigned to feature more free-response questions. Similarly, many undergraduate, graduate, and professional programs place great emphasis upon the personal statements required for admissions to ensure a minimum level of competency. Even in jobs that don't require much formal education, people are now more likely to email or text one another instead of conversing face to face. More and more, communication to carry out personal business or simply socialize is handled in writing in the form of texts or email. Rest assured that you are being critically evaluated when you do so.

Perhaps this is why many people feel uncomfortable writing anything they know will be read by someone else, whether it is a research paper, a cover letter, or a project proposal. A central principle of this book is that clear, organized, and effective writing is highly achievable when you put in a little time, effort, and practice.

The key components of good writing are clarity and honesty. Clarity is for your reader. Unless you write clearly and coherently, your reader will wander from sentence to sentence, never fully grasping your point. Honesty is for you. You will write better when you understand what you are writing.

Why The Princeton Review?

We are the leader in test preparation. Each year we help more than two million students through our courses, online student services and products, and best-selling books. Whether you're looking for help choosing the right college or trying to get a good score on a standardized test like the SAT, ACT, GRE, or MCAT, we're here to make it happen.

Our approach is simple: we teach what you need to know and try to make it interesting and fun at the same time. In preparing students for various standardized tests, we spend much of our time helping students develop practical writing skills, including knowledge of key grammar rules and vocabulary. The ability to express your ideas clearly and succinctly in a written format is essential, regardless of your profession or discipline.

How to Use This Book

Writing Smart covers a variety of writing, from research papers to professional letters, breaking down the writing process into straightforward steps. In short, do what works for you. Here's a chapter-by-chapter breakdown of this book so you know what to expect:

- Chapters 1 through 4 cover the building blocks of writing, beginning with some basic tips for getting ready to write, followed by brief lessons on basic grammar and punctuation rules, as well as words and how to put them together to make well-constructed sentences.

- Chapters 5 through 10 each focus on a different type of writing. Each chapter outlines a step-by-step process, provides you with editing drills as well as writing samples. At the end of each chapter is specific formatting information that you can use for your own writing projects, and a list of recommended reading.

- Finally, the Appendix contains helpful reference information, including a glossary of key terms covered in the book, a list of common grammar errors to avoid when writing, and frequently asked questions related to the subjects of writing and grammar.

With this said, there's no right way to read this book. If you feel you already have a solid grasp of grammar and just want to focus on writing research papers, skip to that chapter. If you're great at writing research papers but need help starting an essay, head over to the chapter on personal essays. And if you have no problem at all with academic assignments but are completely stumped when it comes to writing cover letters, focus on the chapter on professional writing. Do what works for you.

Note that this book covers nonfiction writing only. If you are interesting in learning about fiction writing, we recommend *The Art of Fiction* by John Gardner.

Writing means getting words on paper, and good writing means getting words on paper clearly. Once you understand this distinction, you are on your way to better prose. Working through this book will improve your writing, but your instruction should not end there. The other sure way to improve your writing is to read more! The more you read, the more you'll understand how writing works, and you'll notice certain patterns and rhythms in writing that you can learn to replicate with practice.

Now off we go!

CHAPTER 1

Getting Ready to Write

The Pre-Writing Process

Writing often requires a bit of "pre-work." Once you know what you need to write, you have to prepare, which might mean creating an outline or simply jotting down some notes on paper to organize your thoughts. You don't necessarily need to write down every detail; often, the process of writing will help you discover exactly what you want to say and refine your thoughts. Still, having a general plan will help keep your writing organized and to the point. This chapter covers a few aspects of the pre-writing process.

Do Your Research

If your writing includes research, it is best to get a substantial chunk of the research done before you begin writing (we know you know, just a little reminder). Often information you discover as you research will alter what you might have written, so avoid endless revisions and get as much information as you can, first.

Make an Outline

If you are writing anything longer than a paragraph, it is advisable to construct an outline. An outline describes paragraph by paragraph what you intend to say; it gives you a plan for your writing, so you can chart the beginning, middle, and end of your piece. Of course, no law says that you must follow your outline down to the last detail. The process of writing can give you new ideas of what to write next, so you may want to revise your outline as you go along. Outlines will be covered in more detail in the chapter on research papers.

Set Guidelines for Yourself

There will be a million reasons to get up once you sit down, "Oh, I need more paper, or a new pen, or a towel to wipe off my computer screen." While it is absolutely fine to take breaks when writing, jumping up every five seconds is not helpful to your momentum. Have what you need at hand, and make your surroundings pleasant enough that you might want to stay there for a few hours.

One of the most challenging aspects of writing is getting yourself to sit down and write. There are a few techniques you might try to ensure you keep working to get words on the page. You might, for example, try giving yourself small rewards in exchange for making some progress with your writing: "If I write five pages I'll treat myself to a movie." You might also try asking your friends to hold you accountable. It's said that Ernest Hemingway actually paid his friends to force him to write for two hours every morning.

We recommend that you make a schedule for yourself depending on whatever it is that you're writing. For longer writing tasks like a research paper, dedicate an hour or two a day to writing, preferably at the time of day when you are most productive. Long-form writing is usually best done in shorter spurts in order to keep you focused and motivated. However, a schedule can work just as well in situations where a deadline is fast approaching and you need to keep writing. Break up your time into intervals: writing intervals and break intervals. Write for an hour, and then take a short break to stretch, get some fresh air, or have a snack.

Write Something Down

The writing process entails constant revision and reworking. However, revision can only happen when you have something to revise. Get your thoughts out as they occur to you, even if they are not in the form of perfectly constructed sentences. During the pre-writing process, you should not strive for perfection—you'll have plenty of time to refine your thoughts later on. Just get the sentences down on paper (or on your computer screen).

> **"I'm writing a first draft and reminding myself that I'm just shoveling sand into a box so that later I can build castles."**
>
> **—Shannon Hale**

And that's it. Don't agonize over how to begin. Simply write a sentence. Good or bad, that sentence will start you on the road to completion.

CHAPTER 2

Grammar Basics: A Quick Review

Grammar: What You Need to Know

A common pitfall when it comes to writing is grammar. Those of you who have been out of school for some time may have forgotten some or most of the rules at one point drilled into you by your English teachers. And even if you're a student and are very familiar with grammatical conventions, you may find it difficult to follow them in an increasingly digital world ruled by texting and emojis. So, we get it. But when it comes to formal writing, good grammar is key. Incorrect grammar in writing is distracting; moreover, it can almost immediately discredit you to your reader. So if you want your reading audience to remain engaged and take you seriously, you're going to have to have a solid, fundamental knowledge of parts of speech and punctuation and how to use them correctly. Let's get started.

First up, here is a list of terms with which you should be familiar. Parts of speech and punctuation are the building blocks of writing. Every time you write, you are working with parts of speech, arranging your sentences according to parts of speech. This chapter is designed to broaden your already intuitive knowledge of grammar and punctuation and make it a little more useful to you as you set out to write.

Take a moment to read through the following terms and circle any that you feel you need to review. These terms are also found in the glossary at the end of this book.

Adjective: A word that modifies a noun or pronoun

Adverb: A word that modifies a verb, adjective, or other adverb

Clause: A group of words that contains a subject and a predicate

Colon: A punctuation mark used to introduce a list or amplify the preceding thought

Comma: A punctuation mark used to separate words within a sentence

Dependent Clause: A clause that cannot stand alone as a sentence

Independent Clause: A clause that can stand alone as a sentence

Modifier: A word or group of words in a sentence that limits or qualifies another word or group of words

Noun: A word that represents a person, place, thing, or idea

Parentheses: Punctuation marks used to set off a qualifying or explanatory remark from the rest of the text

Phrase: A group of words that does not contain a subject and verb but which functions as a conceptual unit within a sentence

Pronoun: A word that replaces a noun or noun phrase

Semicolon: A punctuation mark used to separate independent clauses

Sentence: A grammatically independent group of words, usually containing a subject and a predicate, that expresses a statement, command, request, exclamation, etc.

Subject: The person, place, thing, or idea that the sentence is about; the subject performs the action or does the "being"

Verb: A word that expresses action or a state of being

Parts of Speech: The Basics

Determining parts of speech is nothing more than determining the function particular words have in a sentence. Different words, or groups of words, have different functions, and you will be able to avoid making grammatical errors if you are a whiz at determining parts of speech. To build something, you need proper materials; to understand parts of speech is to understand the materials of making sentences—but more on that in Chapter 3. For now, let's go over some basic parts of speech in more detail.

Nouns

Nouns are "person, place, thing, and idea" words. It is easy to see that objects are nouns, and qualities and ideas can be nouns too—*love* is a noun, as is *egotism,* and *spoilage.* Nouns can be singular, as when you are talking about one thing (*box*), or plural, when you're talking about more than one thing (*boxes*). Being able to spot nouns is important because the subject of a sentence is always a noun or a pronoun (we'll cover pronouns in a little while).

Quick Quiz #1

Circle the nouns in the following paragraph. Answers can be found on page 47.

Jimmy Brooks and Casey Jones are the hosts of a wonderful free showcase at Blast Masters Club featuring the best musicians based in the Kansas City area. Although they don't play any instruments, Jimmy and Casey are great at off-the-cuff banter. The musicians featured are the cream of the crop, and the headliner is a lady who uses the stage name Tooth Fairy. She is a hard rocker who hails from New York City and she never lets you forget that she's from the Big Apple. She has known Jimmy and Casey for over fifteen years, and they typically all spend Sundays hanging out at a diner ten minutes away from the club.

Rules for Nouns

1. If you aren't sure whether a word is a noun, put *a* or *the* in front of the word. If it makes sense, then the word is a noun; for example, *a mistake, the mood, the danger.*

2. Proper nouns are names of people, specific places, and particular groups and events. Proper nouns are always capitalized: LeBron James; Paris, France; Central Intelligence Agency; the War of the Roses.

3. Often, a word or group of words that looks like a verb acts as a noun. For example:

   > *Skiing* is Wanda's favorite sport.

   > *To know* me is to love me.

Adjectives

Adjectives are descriptive words. *Gorgeous, hideous, smelly, baggy,* and *pathetic* are all adjectives. They describe or modify nouns. Less obviously descriptive are adjectives that show which one or how many: *that* man, *his* dessert, *enough* meatloaf, *every* dog. See how the adjectives clarify which noun (or how many of each noun) is being talked about?

Rules for Adjectives

1. An adjective like *smart* can be relative; in other words, you aren't necessarily smart or not smart—you can be smart to degrees. To show this kind of comparison, there are three forms of adjectives:

Positive	Comparative	Superlative
smart	smarter	smartest

   - If you are comparing two things, form the comparative by adding *–er* to the adjective.

- If you are comparing more than two things, form the superlative by adding –*est* to the adjective.

- Some adjectives do not lend themselves to adding –*er* or –*est* to the stem. In these cases, use *more* as the comparative and *most* as the superlative. Your ear should be able to discern with form is appropriate. When in doubt, use *more* or *most.*

2. Some adjectives are absolute—you either have the quality or you don't. So there is no comparative or superlative form for adjectives like *complete, final, square, meaningless, superior, dead, unique, universal,* and so on.

3. Adjectives that describe how much or how many are often misused. If you are writing about something that you can count individually, use *fewer* or *many.* If you are writing about something that cannot be counted individually, use *less, a lot of,* or *much.*

Quick Quiz #2

Circle the appropriate adjective. Answers can be found on page 47.

1. Last night I ate (fewer, less) marshmallows than Wanda did.

2. She considered the marshmallow to be (a perfect, the most perfect) food.

3. In rating marshmallows and oysters, Wanda liked marshmallows (best, better).

4. "A marshmallow is (spongier than, the spongiest of) any other food," she said.

5. Although she ate (many, much) marshmallows, she ate (fewer, less) Jell-O.

Verbs

Without a verb, you have no sentence. Verbs express either action (like *hit, sprint,* or *touch*) or state of being (like *am, seems, will be*). The first kind of verb is called an **action verb;** the second kind is called a **linking verb.** This distinction is not anything to worry about; we only mention it to show the various functions of different kinds of verbs. Put another way, a verb tells what the subject is doing or what is being done to the subject, even if the subject is doing nothing more than just existing. The rules for verbs chiefly concern two characteristics: **tense** and **agreement with the subject.**

Tense

The tense of a verb places the action at a particular time. The English language has twelve tenses altogether, so we are able to be quite precise in explaining when something happened. Although memorizing the names of the tenses is not terribly important, you do want to understand which moment in time each tense refers to.

The six basic tenses are:

1. **present:** I eat
2. **present perfect:** I have eaten
3. **past:** I ate
4. **past perfect:** I had eaten
5. **future:** I will eat
6. **future perfect:** I will have eaten

Now let's take a look at what moment in time each tense indicates.

Present: The "now" tense. Use present tense if...

- The action is happening right now: I *am* hungry (right now).

- The action happens habitually: I *am* hungry every afternoon.

- You are stating a fact: Bob Dylan *is* a great songwriter.

- You want dramatic effect in fiction or in expository writing: The phone *rings*. Fitzgerald *is* more interesting than Hemingway. (This use of the present is called the historical present.)

- You are speaking about the future: She *leaves* for Paris in the morning.

Present Perfect: Use present perfect if...

- The action started in the past and continues into the present moment: I *have eaten* sixteen cookies so far this week.

- The action was finished at some point earlier in time but affects the present: I *have eaten* all of the pie, so there isn't any left for you.

Past: The "before" tense. Use the past tense if...

- The action happened in the past and does not continue to happen: I *ate* it.

Past Perfect: The "even before before" tense. Use the past perfect if...

- You are discussing an action already in the past and you need to make clear that another action happened even earlier. Think of past perfect as the double past tense: Before I *ate* your dessert, I *had eaten* 87 doughnuts. (*Ate* is past tense, *had eaten* is past perfect.)

- You have an "if" clause followed by the conditional (would) and the present perfect: *If* I *had thought* about it first, I *would not have eaten* all of those doughnuts.

Future: The *Star Trek* tense. All statements using future tense have not yet happened—they are in the future. Use the future tense if...

- You are writing about something that will happen in the future: Tomorrow *I will* go on a diet.

Future Perfect: This tense combines future and past—and it doesn't come up very often. Use future perfect if...

- An action is finished before a specified time in the future: By next week, I *will have lost* ten pounds.

In addition to these six tenses are the continuous (or progressive) forms of all six. As with the whole subject of tenses, the names of the tenses are not important—what is important is being able to use the right tense in the right situation.

The continuous tenses use the *–ing* verb, or **present participle**: *I am eating, I was eating, I will be eating.* Use the continuous form if you want to show continuous action: I *will be dieting* for eternity.

The **past participle** is the form of the verb that goes with *have* to form the present perfect: *have walked, have sworn, have loved.*

One last term you should know concerning verbs is the **infinitive,** which is simply the "to" form of the verb, as in *to go, to do, to see.*

Deciding on the right verb form presents no problem if the verb is regular. A regular verb is conjugated like any other regular verb:

I move, I moved, I am moving, I have moved

I walk, I walked, I am walking, I have walked

The trouble arises when the verb is irregular, meaning it doesn't fit into the pattern of an added *–ed* to make the past tense and past participle: I walk*ed*, I have walk*ed*. Many irregular verbs—like the verb *to be*— are used so frequently that their irregularity is not a problem, because you know the principal parts by heart, even if you'd never heard of the term principal parts before opening this book.

Principal Parts

present	past	past participle
bear	bore	borne
blow	blew	blown
bring	brought	brought (*not brang*)
creep	crept	crept
dive	dived	dived (*dove* only informally; not *diven*)
drag	dragged	dragged
draw	drew	drawn
drink	drank	drunk
freeze	froze	frozen
get	got	got, gotten
grow	grew	grown
hang	hung	hung (as in *I hung a picture on the wall*)
hang	hanged	hanged (as in *The man was hanged at sunrise*)

present	past	past participle
lay	laid	laid (as in *I laid the book on the bed*)
lend	lent	lent
lie	lay	lain (as in *I have lain in bed all day*)
ring	rang	rung
shake	shook	shaken
shrink	shrank, shrunk	shrunk, shrunken
sink	sank	sunk (not *sinked*)
slay	slew	slain
spring	sprang, sprung	sprung
swear	swore	sworn
swim	swam	swum
tear	tore	torn
weep	wept	wept
wring	wrung	wrung

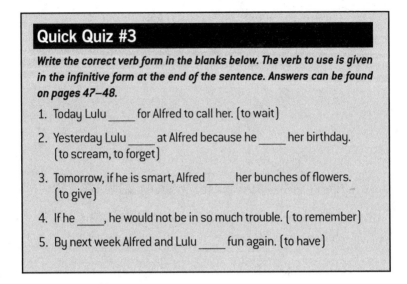

Subject-Verb Agreement

The other main rules concerning verbs involve agreement with their subjects. The number one rule of subject-verb agreement is

---

**Singular subjects take singular verbs,
and plural subjects take plural verbs.**

Here are four easy steps for getting this right when it comes to writing:

1. **Find the main verb.** Don't be distracted by verbal phrases, which are verb-like elements acting as another part of speech.

2. **Ask yourself: Who or what is doing the action?** The answer to this question will be the subject. The subject does not necessarily come before the verb, and there may be all kinds of distracting modifiers and prepositional phrases in between the subject and the verb. Bracket such phrases so that you can see the subject more clearly.

3. **Determine if the subject is singular or plural.** Most of the time, a plural subject will end in –s, though there are plenty of exceptions. You may also need to consider the intended meaning of the word.

4. **Match the subject.** If your subject is singular, match *it* with the correct verb. If your subject is plural, match *they* with the correct verb. You should be able to conjugate this correctly just using your ear.

Basic Rules for Subject-Verb Agreement

- Subjects connected by *and* are plural.

   Bob *and* Sam *are* here.

- Certain expressions (*as well as, including, together with, with,* etc.) logically seem to change a singular subject to plural. They don't. These expressions will be set off from the subject by commas.

   Bob, *along with* Sam and Harry, *is* going on vacation.

- Singular subjects connected by conjunctions such as *either-or, neither-nor,* and *nor* stay singular.

   Neither Bob *nor* Harry *is* able to get up from the sofa.

- If a singular and plural subject are connected by *either-or, neither-nor,* or *nor,* the verb should agree with the subject closes to it.

   Neither Bob nor *the others were* able to get up from the sofa.

   Neither the others nor *Bob was* able to get up from the sofa.

Adverbs

Adverbs modify verbs (run *quickly*), adjectives (*often* happy), or other adverbs (*too* quickly). Adverbs frequently end in *–ly,* but the *–ly* isn't a requirement. A test for determining adverbs is to think about unction: adverbs tend to tell where, when, or how.

Possible Confusion: Adjectives also modify, so it is easy to confuse them with adverbs. And even more confusingly, some words sometimes act as adjectives and sometimes act as adverbs, depending on the sentence and the circumstance. Ask yourself which word is being described: adjectives always modify nouns or pronouns, an adverbs never do.

Rules for Adverbs

1. Adverbs follow the same form as adjectives when they are used to make comparisons.

Positive	Comparative	Superlative
soon	sooner	soonest
little	less	least

2. In placing adverbs, follow this simple rule: put the adverb as close as possible to the word being modified. Otherwise, you may end up giving your sentence a meaning other than the one you intend. For example:

    > My headache was *only* temporary.

    > *Only* my headache was temporary.

    How does the meaning of the sentence change when the adverb is moved?

Pronouns

Pronouns are a subgroup of nouns; they act as stand-ins for nouns. There are eight categories of pronouns, but a few simple rules govern their use. First, let's go over some terms.

- **Case** refers to the function of the pronoun in the sentence. The three cases are nominative, objective, and possessive. Think of these as subject pronouns, object pronouns, and ownership pronouns.
- **Number** makes a pronoun either singular or plural.
- **Gender** specifies whether the person a pronoun refers to is a man or a woman.
- An **antecedent** is the noun (usually appearing earlier in the sentence or paragraph than the pronoun) that the pronoun stands in for in the sentence.

Personal Pronouns

Subject pronouns (nominative case): *I, you, he, she, it, we,* and *they.* All of these serve as the subject of a verb.

> *It* is alive! (*It* is the subject of *is*)

> Wanda knew exactly what *she* should do. (*she* is the subject of *should do*)

Object pronouns (objective case): *me, you, him, her, it, us, them.* These are always the object of the verb, preposition, or infinitive—never the subject. In other words, object pronouns are having something done to them, rather than doing the action themselves.

> Wanda showered *him* with insults. (The *him* isn't doing anything— he's receiving the insults, not showering them.)

> He wanted *her* to go to a movie with *him*. (*He* is the subject of *wanted*; *her* is the object of *wanted*; *him* is the object of the preposition *with*.)

Ownership pronouns (possessive case): *mine, yours, his, hers, its, ours, theirs.* They are used to show ownership, answering the question "Whose?"

The dog was *hers.* (Whose dog? *Her* dog)

There are many other types of pronouns, including mirror pronouns, relative pronouns, question pronouns, pointing pronouns, and indefinite pronouns, all of which are beyond the focus of this book For more pronoun help, we encourage you to check out *Grammar Smart,* our guide for all things grammar.

Prepositions

Prepositions express relationships between other words, usually nouns, including relationships of time or space. *In, of, to,* and *with* are all prepositions. A helpful trick to determine whether a word is a preposition is to place it before "the fence."

Beyond the fence, *past* the fence, *over* the fence, *under* the fence, *of* the fence, *across* the fence—all of these constructions make some kind of sense, so all the italicized words are prepositions, just doing their job: defining relationships. "The fence" is the object of the preposition.

Other prepositions include:

- across
- after
- at
- as
- before
- between
- by
- for
- from
- in
- like
- of
- on
- over
- through
- to
- under
- until
- up
- with

Rules for Prepositions

1. Use *between* when you're writing about two things or groups; use *among* for more than two things.

> Sydney couldn't decide *between* the motorcycle and the Jet Ski.

> The lottery prize was divided among the three winners.

2. A commonly heard grammatical rule is: don't end a sentence with a proposition. Well, maybe, maybe not. If you want to sound formal—for a paper at school or a memo at work—put the preposition in the middle of the sentence and add a word such as *which* or *whom*.

> I picked up a rock *with which* to hit him.

As opposed to the more informal,

> I picked up a rock to hit him *with*.

The content of the sentence may indicate the better choice. If putting the preposition in the middle of the sentence sounds awkward, just leave it at the end.

Quick Quiz #4

Underline the prepositional phrases in the following passage. Answers can be found on page 48.

Billy was not exactly Mr. Popularity at school. Like many American schools, Hoover High was divided into cliques: the jocks and cheerleaders, the artsy people, ruffians, and timid people. Billy was a member of none of them; he was in his own clique, which is an accomplishment in itself, since a clique, by definition, is a group. In fact, Billy was not just Billy, because he was destined for something more dramatic than anything even the theater people could ever have imagined. He was not just Billy, Young Teen. He was, in some hidden way, being prepared for a visit from the alien.

Conjunctions

Conjunctions connect words or parts of sentences—*conjoin* means to join together. There are three categories of conjunctions: coordinating conjunctions, correlative conjunctions, and subordinating conjunctions.

Also known as matchmaking conjunctions, **coordinating conjunctions** connect equal parts of sentences. In other words, they connect words to words, phrases to phrases, and clauses to clauses.

Wanda *and* Max were late to the party. (noun to noun)

Wanda spent the day playing the sax *or* walking the dog. (phrase to phrase)

Max hated his job, *but* he couldn't afford to quit. (clause to clause)

Coordinating Conjunctions:

and	nor
or	so
but	yet
for	

Correlative conjunctions, or seesaw conjunctions, connect equal parts together. The difference between these and coordinating conjunctions is that correlative conjunctions are really two conjunctions in one.

Either *Wanda* or *Max would get promoted.*

Wanda wanted not only *fame and riches* but also *love.*

Correlative Conjunctions:

both-and	neither-nor
either-or	not only-but also

Finally, **subordinating conjunctions,** also known as linking conjunctions, connect dependent (subordinate) clauses with the independent, or main, clause. Subordinate clauses act as nouns or adverbs.

Max quit his job *because* he was bored.

He later realized he should have waited *until* he had a new job.

Now he had to decide *what to do next.*

Because he was bored answers the question *Why did Max quit?* so the clause is functioning as an adverb. *Until he had a new job* answers the question *How long should Max have waited?* so it, too, is an adverb clause. *What to do next* answers the question *What did Max have to decide?* so it is a noun clause. These clauses aren't sentences themselves—they can't stand alone. They need to be connected to the main clauses *Max quit his job* and *He later realized he should have waited.* The linking conjunction acts as the link, connecting the subordinate clause to the main clause.

Subordinating Conjunctions:

after	except that	unless
although as	ever since	until
as if	if	when
as long as	if only	whenever
because	in case	where
before	just as	wherever
but that	since	while
even if		

Articles

Articles introduce nouns: *the* is a definite article, *a* and *an* are indefinite articles. Try using them in a sentence to understand the distinction between definite and indefinite.

A mouse could be any mouse, anywhere.

The mouse specifies definitely—the mouse in my room, for example.

Articles have a simple function—to point out, or introduce, a noun. Think of them as adjectives, since they are really describing the nouns they introduce.

Punctuation: The Basics

It's time to deal with those tiny scratch-marks known as punctuation. Like syntax, punctuation can be part of a writer's style; in some instances, the rules are fuzzy enough that a writer can choose his or her manner of punctuating to suit his or her purpose. Hemingway, to go back to our example in the introduction, was a big fan of the period. Simple sentence, period. Henry James, on the other hand, needed dozens of semicolons and thousands of commas, parentheses, and dashes just to get through one sentence.

The purpose of punctuation is to make the act of reading your sentences easier and to make the movement of the eye across the page smoother. The purpose of punctuation is not to draw attention to itself—you want the reader to pay attention to what you have written, not to the placement of commas. Try to cultivate a natural, easygoing punctuation style. If you happen to read something in which the punctuation seems irritating, take a minute to figure out what, precisely, seems bothersome about it.

This section is not meant to be complete; it covers basic rules, common confusions, and common errors.

The Period

The period signals a full stop.

Rules for Periods

1. Put a period at the end of a sentence.

2. Put a period after most abbreviations: Mr. Wifflamoo, Mrs. Smith, Pres. Obama, Nov. 12, A.M., etc. Some abbreviations don't need periods: FBI, NBC, JFK (government organizations, networks, monograms).

3. Put a period outside parentheses if what is enclosed by parentheses is not a complete sentence (like this). (Put a period at the end of a complete sentence enclosed by parentheses.)

4. Put a period inside quotation marks: The sign said "No Admittance."

The Question Mark

A question mark signals that the preceding statement is a question.

Rules for Question Marks

1. Use a question mark at the end of a question sentence.

    Does this look like the correct place for a question mark?

    Is it love?

2. If the question is a quotation, put quotation marks after the question mark.

> He asked, "May I have this dance?"

> "How do I look?" she asked.

3. If the question is not part of the quotation, put the question mark after the quotation marks.

> What do you think of "No new taxes"?

> Do you believe in "an eye for an eye"?

The Exclamation Point

Exclamation points are used for emphasis! Excitement! Surprise!

Rules for Exclamation Points

1. Use an exclamation point after an exclamation.

> Get lost!

> Aha!

> We won!

2. Don't get carried away with exclamation points. The only error generally committed is using an exclamation point to try to give writing more emphasis than it deserves. Use them sparingly!!!

The Comma

The comma is the most abused punctuation mark, possibly because writers are sometimes so worried about following rules that they forget to pay attention to the way the words sound when spoken. Commas help a reader understand the rhythm of the sentence. If you are having comma problems, try saying your sentence out loud and listening for natural pauses. The function of a comma is to slow the reader down briefly—to make the reader pause. The omission of a comma can allow phrases and clauses to crash into one another, thereby confusing the reader.

Commas can influence the meaning of your sentence. Consider the following:

> Although I wanted to kill Max, I controlled myself.

> Although I wanted to kill, Max, I controlled myself.

In the first sentence Max is the person I wanted to kill; in the second sentence I am talking to Max about my desire to kill something else. The comma controls the meaning.

Let's look at another:

> The food tastes terrible, however the cook fixes it.

> The food tastes terrible; however, the cook fixes it.

In the first sentence, the food tastes terrible no matter how the cook fixes it. In the second sentence, the cook improves the taste of the food. Again, the comma controls the meaning.

Rules for Commas

1. Use a comma to separate two independent clauses connected by conjunctions: *and, but, or, nor, for.*

    > Bob was usually a quiet man, *but* he screamed upon entering the room.

The strange man lying under the table appeared to be dead, *or* just possibly he was only napping.

If the independent clauses are short, you may omit the comma.

The man was still and his foot was bleeding.

His hat was on but his pants were off.

2. Use a comma to separate elements in a list or series; the comma is a substitute for *and*. Some people omit the final comma, but we prefer to leave it in.

Bob tried to breathe, to keep from fainting, and to remember his first aid.

Next to the man was a bassoon, a water balloon, and a raccoon.

3. Use a comma to separate introductory phrases and clauses from the independent clause.

After catching his breath, Bob squatted next to the man and took his pulse.

When he felt sad, Bob picked up the bassoon and blew.

Although he had never played a bassoon before, he somehow managed to make beautiful music.

If the introductory phrase is short, you may omit the comma.

After dark they stopped playing basketball.

But be careful. Always use a comma if omitting it could cause confusion.

When Bob began to eat, rats ran across the carpet.

Not: When Bob began to eat rats ran across the carpet.

Before leaving, Bob heard the man sneeze.

Not: Before leaving Bob heard the man sneeze.

4. In a series of adjectives, use a comma if the adjectives could also be separated by *and*.

    The nimble, fat raccoon began to poke at the water balloon.

    Or: The nimble and fat raccoon...

If the *and* doesn't fit, leave out the comma:

    The man's white cotton shirt was balled up in a corner.

    Not: The man's white and cotton shirt...

If this rule seems confusing, try reading the sentence aloud. If you make a slight pause between adjectives, put in commas. Otherwise, leave them out. Another test: if you can change the order of the adjectives, put in commas. For example:

    The handsome, brilliant scholar

    Or: The brilliant, handsome scholar

    The frilly party dress

    Not: The party frilly dress

The final comma in a list is called the Oxford comma (or Harvard comma or serial/series comma). Most grammarians have a particular affinity for the Oxford comma due to its ability to clear up ambiguity. Others argue that it's superfluous because the coordinating conjunction connecting the last two items in a list is enough to keep the parts of the list separate. It's all a matter of preference. Most people are happy using it, but in some arenas it's avoided. Journalistic writing discourages use of the serial comma, and British culture tends to shy away as well. However, standard American writing conventions include consistent use of a final comma in a list. Therefore, gauge your audience, make necessary adjustments, and keep ambiguity minimal.

5. Use commas to set off clauses, but don't use commas for defining clauses. (Quick review: a defining, or restrictive, clause is one that can't be left out of a sentence. Clauses that don't define can be lifted from the sentence without changing the meaning. Also, a defining clause specifies which part of a larger group we are talking about.)

> Bananas that are green taste tart.
> (*that are green* defines which bananas we mean)

> Bananas, which grow in the tropics, do not need refrigeration. (*which grow in the tropics* refers to all bananas. The clause can be lifted from the sentence without changing the meaning.)

Let's look at a sentence you could punctuate either way, depending on the meaning.

> The men who were tired and hungry began eating sardines. (*who were tired and hungry* is a defining clause, telling us which men we mean)

> The men, who were tired and hungry, began eating sardines. (*who were tired and hungry* describes all of the men, and doesn't differentiate these men from other men who weren't tired and hungry)

6. Words or phrases that interrupt the sentence should be set off by commas.

> Now then, let's get down to work.

> "Help me," he said, before falling down the stairs.

> What the candidate promised, in fact, is impossible to achieve.

> Hello, I must be going.

7. Use commas to set off an appositive. An appositive is a word or phrase that explains or introduces the noun that precedes it.

> Mrs. Bowden, my favorite teacher, is wearing a hat.

> Ralphie, the president of the student council, is on probation.

Remember that commas are one way to make your writing clear. Reading your sentences aloud is a very good way to find the natural place for commas, as is inspecting your sentences for ambiguity or confusion.

The Semicolon

For some reason, the semicolon is the most feared punctuation mark; it seems to inspire loss of confidence in even the most accomplished writers. The rules for semicolons are simple.

Rules for Semicolons

1. Use a semicolon to link two independent clauses.

> To give a good party, you must consider the lighting; no one feels comfortable under the bright glare of fluorescent lights.

Note that the two clauses are connected in thought. Also—and this is the thing to understand about semicolons—you could use a comma and a conjunction in place of the semicolon.

> To give a good party, you must consider the lighting, *since* no one feels comfortable under the bright glare of fluorescent lights.

2. Use a semicolon to separate elements in a list if the elements are long or if the elements themselves have commas in them.

> To get completely ready for your party, you should clean your house; make sure your old, decrepit stereo works; prepare a lot of delicious, strange food; and expect odd, antisocial, or frivolous behavior on the part of your guests.

3. Semicolons belong outside quotation marks.

> One man at the party sat in a corner and read "The Adventures of Bob"; he may have been shy, or he may have found "The Adventures of Bob" too exciting to put down.

The Colon

A colon tells a reader to pay attention to what follows.

Rules for Colons

1. Use a colon when making a list.

> There are four ingredients necessary to a good party: music, lighting, food, and personality.

2. A colon is sometimes used to introduce a quotation or an explanation.

> On Saturday President Obama made the following statement: "This country's economy can be revived!"

3. A colon must follow an independent clause that makes the reader or listener expect more information to follow.

Parentheses

Rules for Parentheses

1. Use parentheses to enclose extra material (explanations, asides, and so on) that would otherwise interrupt the flow of the sentence.

    > If you go skin diving at night (an adventure for only the most experienced divers), you can observe strange and amazing phenomena.

    > As she whipped the cream (after making sure the ingredients were very cold), she told us she had made mousse only once before.

2. Put a period inside the parentheses if what is inside the parentheses is a complete sentence. (See Rules for Periods, on page 25.)

3. Don't put a comma after the parentheses unless the sentence would require it anyway.

The Dash

Dashes can be used in place of a colon or parentheses. Some people feel that dashes signify greater emphasis. Whether you use dashes is your choice—they are optional.

Rules for Dashes

1. Use one dash in place of a colon, following the rules for colons.

    > We finished our tasks in record time—one hour!

    > **Or:** We finished our tasks in record time: one hour!

2. You can use dashes instead of parentheses.

> If you come to my house—take a left after crossing the bridge—please bring some turnips and an oboe.

> **Or:** If you come to my house (take a left after crossing the bridge) please bring some turnips and an oboe.

The Apostrophe

The apostrophe is used to show ownership. Most of the time, it presents no confusion: Bob's bassoon, the woman's finger. The tricky part is using an apostrophe when the owner is plural.

Rules for Apostrophes

1. If the plural noun doesn't end in –s, add an apostrophe and –s. (This is the easy part.)

> the women's fingers

> the bacteria's growth

> the cat's hairballs

2. If the plural ends in –s, just add an apostrophe.

> the babies' bottoms

> the horses' hooves

> the politicians' promises

3. If the word is a proper noun that ends in –s, add an apostrophe and an –s. (This is the part people get wrong.)

> Yeats's poem

> Ross's riddle

> Chris's crisis

4. One exception is the possessive of the pronoun *it*, which is *its* (no apostrophe). The word *it's* (with apostrophe) is the contraction for *it is*, not the possessive.

> We're giving the robot *its* weekly check-up today.

> **Not:** We're giving the robot *it's* weekly check-up today.

> *It's* a beautiful day in the neighborhood.

> **Not:** *Its* a beautiful day in the neighborhood.

If this strikes you as confusing, notice that the word *it* is treated similarly to the words *he*, *she*, and *they*. When apostrophes are added to these words, they become contractions: *he's* going to the store, *she's* going to bed, and *they're* going to work. The possessive pronouns do not contain apostrophes: *his* book, *her* food, *their* table, *its* mountains. If you're still confused, say the sentence out loud. You're not giving the robot *it is* weekly check-up, are you?

The Hyphen

A hyphen separates compound words. In etymological evolution, two words may be separate, then joined by a hyphen, then joined together. For instance, *week end* changed to *week-end* and then to *weekend*. The best way to find out about a particular word is to look it up in the dictionary.

Rules for Hyphens

1. If the pair of words forms an adjective that comes before the noun, use a hyphen.

> well-known felon

> first-class work

2. If the adjective pair comes after the noun, you don't need a hyphen.

> His crimes are well known.

> His work is always first class.

3. Use a hyphen for fractions acting as adjectives:

> He drank one and two-thirds cans of soda.

But not for fractions acting as nouns:

> Two thirds of the people have gone home.

4. Use a hyphen to differentiate certain words:

> He recollected his adventure in Guam.

> He re-collected the money.

> She recovered from the flu.

> She re-covered the sofa.

Quotation Marks

The main problem with quotation marks is knowing whether other punctuation marks belong inside or outside of them. For periods, commas, and question marks, look back in this section to A, B, and C, respectively.

Rules for Quotation Marks

1. Put quotation marks around direct quotations.

> "Here's Johnny!" said Nicholson.

2. If you have a quote within a quote, put single quotation marks around it.

> "He said, 'I can't live without you.'"

> "Stop!" said Victor, "or I'll yodel 'My Wild Irish Rose.'"

3. The use of quotation marks to show irony has become tired; avoid it if you can. And never, ever use air quotes.

Quick Quiz #5

Punctuate the following passage. Answers can be found on page 48.

Billy had several more visits from the aliens sometimes they ate snacks on his Buick sometimes they played music and danced One alien in particular became Billy's friend The alien taught Billy some good tricks a foolproof method for shooting foul shots a lip smacking recipe for tadpoles and a way to make his eyes change color at will.

Later in life Billy found himself married with two small children living in a peaceful suburb He said that he couldn't be happier

You miss the aliens said his wife one night putting the children to bed

She was right His Buick had long ago gone to the scrap heap and the aliens once his friends did not appear anymore Sometimes it made Billy sad but he threw himself into his work as an accountant for a chain of dry cleaners and occasionally he made a little money making bets on his foul-shooting Although he lived a sedate quiet life he always treasured the days of snacking with the aliens.

Emojis

Thanks to text messaging and emailing, emoticons have become quite popular. Before emojis emerged, emoticons (emotional "faces" derived from combinations of punctuation marks and symbols) were used to express emotions in text that might be misinterpreted or confusing. For example, instead of using all capital letters to express anger or frustration, an angry face could simply emphasize the text and convey the mood. All capital letters could mean excitement, as opposed to anger, so if the face is present in the text, confusion is less likely to occur. While using emojis and emoticons is fun and increasingly socially acceptable, you should understand the importance of appropriate use in both personal and professional settings. ( )

Personal conversations are fairly open for use of symbols simply because the nature of personal relationships allows playfulness even in serious situations. Professional settings require careful consideration, as use of symbols may portray lack of professionalism or respect. ( )

Our suggestion is to consider audience. If you are applying for a job, making a serious statement, or writing to someone with whom you are relatively unfamiliar, steer clear of emojis and other symbols. If your professional relationships are somewhat personal in nature (you've worked there a while; you know your colleagues or your boss outside of work), then consider the content of the correspondence and use symbols appropriately. A smiley face at the end of a "Thank you for the delicious teacher appreciation lunch !" is acceptable.

Our best advice is to be careful, not careless, when using emoticons, emojis, or symbols in written correspondence. ( )

Writing Smart: Grammar Rules You Need to Know

Now that we've gone over some basic parts of speech, let's put them in context. The following are a few important rules concerning grammar that we've already gone over, as well as rules for punctuation and capitalization that you should always remember. By doing so you can avoid the most common English-language pitfalls!

1. **A verb must agree with its subject, regardless of any words that separate the two.**

   Cheddar cheese, which Mickey serves to his friends at all his parties, is his favorite variety.

   Cheddar cheese is a singular noun that requires the singular verb *is*. The plural words *friends* and *parties* within the commas, although potentially confusing, are irrelevant.

2. **Pronouns must agree with the nouns they replace; the pronoun *they* cannot be used with a singular noun to achieve gender neutrality.**

   INCORRECT: A Harvard student must study hard if they want to succeed.

   Student is a singular noun that requires a singular pronoun, not the plural pronoun *they*. *He*, *she*, or *he or she* would all be correct alternatives in a case wherein the gender of the individual is unknown.

3. **Pronouns must have a clear referent and cannot be ambiguous.**

   INCORRECT: I'm going to wear a coat, since they say it will be cold tonight.

   Who precisely are *they*? We have no idea, so the pronoun is ambiguous and therefore incorrect.

INCORRECT: Laverne and Shirley always fight when she is in a bad mood.

They fight when *who* is in a bad mood, Laverne or Shirley? We don't know, so the sentence is incorrect as written.

4. **A comma cannot separate two independent clauses.**

   INCORRECT: I love chocolate, I eat it every chance I get!

   Both clauses could stand alone as sentences here, so a comma cannot be used. This error is known as a **comma splice**. Correct alternatives include dividing the sentence into two sentences with a period, using a semicolon, or adding a conjunction such as *and* or *so* (e.g., I love chocolate and I eat it every chance I get!).

5. **Two independent clauses must be separated by appropriate punctuation.**

   I love New England the towns are so charming!

   I love New England and *the towns are so charming!* can both stand alone as sentences, so they must be separated. This error is known as a **run-on sentence**. Once again, dividing the sentence into two sentences with a period, adding a conjunction, or using a semicolon are correct alternatives (e.g., *I love New England; the towns are so charming!*).

6. **As a general rule, proper nouns should be capitalized and common nouns should be lowercase.**

   What *state* do you live in? I live in *Florida*.

   Do you own a *cat*? Yes, *Dolly* is my cat (or, more accurately, I am her human).

Do you like to study *history*? Yes, I took *History* 301 three times in college.

7. **Regular nouns are pluralized by adding an *s*; an apostrophe and an −*s* indicates possession.**

   INCORRECT: The football player's were running around the field.

   CORRECT: The football players were running around the field.

   CORRECT: The football player's helmet saved him from serious injury.

   CORRECT: The football players' helmets saved them from serious injury.

   Note that you create the possessive form of the plural noun *players* simply by adding an apostrophe.

8. **Homonyms are not interchangeable.**

   Although they are pronounced the same way, **homonyms** have completely different meanings and should never be mistaken for one another. These are a few of the most problematic examples:

   your (second-person possessive pronoun)

   you're (contraction of *you* and *are*)

   You're going to have to improve *your* singing if *you're* ever going to make it in Hollywood.

   its (third-person possessive pronoun)

   it's (contraction of *it* and *is*)

   It's a beautiful sight to see a peacock spread *its* colorful tail feathers.

there ("in or at that place")

they're (contraction of *they* and *are*)

their (third-person plural possessive pronoun)

The Joneses should quickly move *their* car over there or else *they're* surely going to get a ticket.

Now it's time to put your new knowledge to the test in the following series of drills. Answers and explanations are provided at the end of the chapter.

Drill 1

Choose the best answer. If you don't find an error, choose (A).

1. Gomez thought Pinky's hairstyle <u>was the most unique, but whom had designed</u> her hideous dress?

   A) No change

   B) was the most unique, but who designed

   C) to be the most unique, but whom had designed

   D) was unique, but who had been designing

   E) was unique, but who had designed

2. The dresses <u>which hung on the rack were made for Pinky and I</u>.

   A) No change

   B) which hung on the rack were made for Pinky and me

   C) that were hanging on the rack having been made for Pinky and I

   D) that hung on the rack were made for Pinky and me

   E) hanged on the rack and they were made for me and Pinky

3. <u>The one criteria you must meet to dress well is knowing what cut is right for one's body.</u>

   A) No change

   B) To dress well, the one criteria you must meet is to know what cut is right for your body.

   C) In dressing well, the one criterion you must meet is knowing what cut is right for one's body.

   D) To dress well, the one criterion you must meet is to know what cut is right for your body.

   E) The one criterion you must meet, for dressing well, is knowing what cut is right for your body.

4. In 1978, a peak of nonfashion, <u>great amounts of people wear</u> polyester jackets.

   A) No change

   B) great amounts of people were wearing

   C) great numbers of people wore

   D) a great amount of people wore

   E) large numbers of people are wearing

5. Now that it is 2018, pumps and tight jeans <u>will be back on the runway, but her and me have less of these</u> retro items in our closets.

   A) No change

   B) will be back on the runway, but she and me will have fewer of these

   C) are back on the runway, but she and I have fewer of these

   D) are being back on the runway, but she and I have less of these

   E) are back on the runway, but her and I have fewer of these

Drill 2

Circle the error. If you find no error, circle (E).

1. The novelist, the <u>most talented</u> of the two writers <u>who</u> came
   A B

   over for dinner, <u>slipped</u> on a tennis ball <u>that was lying</u> on the
   C D

   rug in the hallway. <u>No change</u>
   E

2. The screenwriter was <u>deliriously happy</u> <u>to see</u> that Pinky and
   A B

   Bob <u>had began</u> to cook the cabbage <u>and grill</u> the steaks.
   C D

   <u>No change</u>
   E

3. <u>That the writers</u> had not been able to afford <u>anything but</u> beans
   A B

   and rice was <u>evident in their delight</u> at sitting down to the feast,
   C

   and in the dangerous speed <u>with which</u> they inhaled their food.
   D

   <u>No change</u>
   E

4. The <u>argument among</u> the two writers <u>was</u> not a scholarly
   A B

   dispute; they were simply <u>trying to divide</u> the last piece of cake
   C

   <u>between them</u>. <u>No change</u>
   D E

5. The novelist, <u>who modeled himself</u> after Hemingway, wrestled
   A

   the cake away from the screenwriter, <u>who was known for</u> <u>constant</u>
   B C

   changing artistic direction; sometimes he <u>wrote like</u> Godard, and
   D

   sometimes like Spielberg. <u>No change</u>
   E

Drill 3

Identify the part of speech of every word in the following sentences.

1. I am shivering from the cold.

2. I made delicious pot roast and beans and rice for dinner.

3. There is nothing better than pot roast, in my opinion.

4. Yikes! I somehow left my hat in the oven!

5. Actually we would rather order Chinese food and watch TV, because we can eat these fortune cookies and stand on our heads until we are ready for bed.

Chapter 1 Answers and Explanations

Quick Quiz #1

Jimmy Brooks, Casey Jones, hosts, showcase, Blast Masters Club, musicians, area, instruments, Jimmy, Casey, banter, musicians, cream of the crop, headliner, lady, stage name, Tooth Fairy, rocker, New York City, Big Apple, Jimmy, Casey, years, Sundays, diner, minutes, club

Quick Quiz #2

1. fewer (individual marshmallows)

2. a perfect (absolute adjective)

3. better (comparing two things)

4. spongier than (comparing a marshmallow to any other single-food: two things)

5. many (individual marshmallows); less (uncountable Jell-O)

Quick Quiz #3

There are several correct answers for some questions in this drill. If you wrote in any of the following you are A-OK:

1. waits, is waiting, waited, was waiting, has waited, has been-waiting, will wait

2. screamed, was screaming; forgot, had forgotten

3. will give

4. had remembered

5. will have, will be having

Quick Quiz #4

at school, into cliques, of none, of them, in his own clique, in itself, by definition, in fact, for something, in some hidden way, for a visit, from the alien

Quick Quiz #5

Billy had several more visits from the aliens. Sometimes they ate snacks on his Buick; sometimes they played music and danced. One alien in particular became Billy's friend. The alien taught Billy some good tricks: a foolproof method for shooting foul shots, a lip smacking recipe for tadpoles, and a way to make his eyes change color at will.

Later in life, Billy found himself married, with two small children, living in a peaceful suburb. He said that he couldn't be happier.

"You miss the aliens," said his wife one night, putting the children to bed.

She was right. His Buick had long ago gone to the scrap heap, and the aliens, once his friends, did not appear anymore. Sometimes it made Billy sad, but he threw himself into his work as an accountant for a chain of dry cleaners and occasionally he made a little money making bets on his foul-shooting. Although he lived a sedate, quiet life, he always treasured the days of snacking with the aliens.

Drill 1

1. **E**   *Unique* is an absolute adjective; you can't be more or less unique. That gets rid of (A), (B), and (C). Choice (D) uses the past perfect continuous (*had been designing*) for no good reason. Past perfect is more appropriate because it makes clear that the dress was designed at an earlier time than Gomez thought.

2. **D**   *That* is better than *which*, because the clause *that were made for Pinky and me* defines which dresses we mean. Also, the clause is not set off by commas, which is another indicator that *which* would not be appropriate. That eliminates (A) and (B). In (C), the clause *having been made* functions as an adjective, leaving the sentence with no verb. Also, in (A) and (C), the pronoun case is incorrect: made for *me*, not made for *I*. Choice (E) is awkward and uses *hanged*, which only applies to people (grotesquely enough), not dresses.

3. **D**   *Criteria* is plural; *criterion* is singular. So (A), (B), and (E) are out. Choice (C) switches from *you* to *one*. Remember to keep pronouns consistent.

4. **C**   *Amount* applies to non-countable nouns, such as water. Cross out (A), (B), and (D). Choice (E) has a tense problem; the sentence is referring to 1978, so you need past tense (wore), not present continuous (are wearing).

5. **C**   Look at the clause *but her and me have*: the verb *have* requires a subject, so *her* or *me* (objective case) is incorrect. Get rid of (A), (B), and (E). Choice (D) says *are being back*, which is nutty. Also, pumps and tight jeans are countable nouns, so *fewer* is appropriate, not *less*.

Drill 2

1. **A** When comparing two nouns, use the comparative form: *more talented*. *Most talented* is the superlative form, used to compare more than two nouns.

2. **C** Wrong principal part. The past participle of *begin* is *begun*.

3. **E** No error.

4. **A** Use *among* for more than two, and *between* for two.

5. **C** *Constant* is an adjective. The word being modified is *changing*, a verb, so you need an adverb: *constantly*.

Drill 3

1.

I	am	shivering	from	the	cold.
PRO	VERB	VERB	PREP	ART	NOUN

2.

I	made	delicious	pot roast	and	beans
PRO	VERB	ADJ	NOUN	CONJ	NOUN

and	rice	for	dinner.
CONJ	NOUN	PREP	NOUN

3.

There	is	nothing	better	than	pot roast,
PRO	VERB	PRO	ADJ	PREP	NOUN

in	my	opinion.
PREP	PRO	NOUN

4.

Yikes!	I	somehow	left	my	hat
INTERJ	PRO	ADV	VERB	ADJ	NOUN

in	the	oven!
PREP	ART	NOUN

5. | Actually, | we | would | rather | order | Chinese |
ADV	PRO	VERB	ADV	VERB	ADJ
food	and	watch	TV,		
NOUN	CONJ	VERB	NOUN		
because	we	can	eat	these	
CONJ	PRO	VERB	VERB	ADJ	
fortune	and	stand	on	our	heads
cookies	CONJ	VERB	PREP	ADJ	NOUN
NOUN					
until	we	are	ready	for	bed.
CONJ	PRO	VERB	ADJ	PREP	NOUN

Note: *Pot roast* and *fortune cookies* may each be thought of as one noun.

CHAPTER 3

Words, Sentences, and Paragraphs

How Words Function

> "What can be said at all, can be said clearly."
>
> —Ludwig Wittgenstein

> "Prefer the familiar word to the far-fetched.
> Prefer the concrete to the abstract. Prefer the
> single word to the circumlocution. Prefer the short
> word to the long."
>
> —H.W. and F.G. Fowler

In the previous chapter, we focused on basic parts of speech and punctuation—the building blocks of writing. But good writing is more than perfect grammar (though that certainly helps). To write well—to engage your reader, further your argument, to make a point, whatever your intention may be—you need to know how those building blocks of the English language can be pulled together to create well-constructed sentences that clearly convey your intended meaning. Part of this involves making the right word choices—using words that are precise and clarify your point rather than obscure or confuse it. That's what this chapter is about: how to use words to construct good sentences, which become well-thought-out paragraphs, which are then joined together to become your completed written work, whether that's a business memo, a research paper, or personal essay.

Words

Here are some fundamental rules regarding word choice that you should follow in any type of formal writing.

1. Stay Away from Slang

Written English has different standards than spoken English. When you are conversing you can amplify your meaning with gestures, facial expressions, tone of voice, and word emphasis. These aids are not available to your written communication. Thus, your written work must be as absolutely clear as you can make it. Some of your readers may be unfamiliar with colloquial uses of certain words, so unless you are going to clearly explain the use of a word in its context, do not use it in a nonstandard way.

2. The Best Word Isn't Always the Biggest Word

"Henceforth I would desire to act in a more extemporaneous manner."

equals

"I want to be more spontaneous."

The perfect word to use is the one that most nearly conveys exactly what you mean. That is, the best word is the most precise word. Do not consult your thesaurus for the largest word you can squeeze into your sentence. In most cases, this will make your sentence awkward and ungainly, and will give your prose a stiff and pretentious air. If the most precise word also happens to be one with many syllables, so be it. But don't use big words just to use them.

3. Avoid Repetition

One use of the thesaurus that is defensible *is* as a means to avoid excessive repetition. Certain words will be repeated in a paper or essay. For example, if your piece is about dogs, it will be difficult to avoid using the word "dog," but avoid repetition when possible.

4. Be Aware of Redundancy

Redundancy involves using more words than necessary to convey meaning. For example, the phrase "free gift" is redundant because gifts, by definition, are free.

Here are a few redundancies that often show up in writing:

the reason why	*instead use*	the reason
very unique	*instead use*	unique
as long or longer than	*instead use*	at least as long
never ever	*instead use*	never

Some other common redundancies include:

- small in size
- circulate around
- true fact
- joint partnership
- close to the point of
- in this day and time
- consensus of opinion
- pair of twins (unless you mean four people)
- cooperate together, collaborate together

- close proximity
- contemporary writer of today
- if and when
- mingle together
- new innovation
- joint cooperation
- 3:00 A.M. in the morning
- 6:00 P.M. at night

Unfortunately, redundancy can crop up anywhere, not just with words but in sentences and paragraphs as well. Unnecessary sentences weaken your writing. Make sure that each word, sentence, and paragraph contributes something essential to the whole. If it does not, omit it.

5. When in Doubt, Use a Dictionary

Do you see the problem with this sign? The correct word to use here is "prosecuted," not "persecuted." When in doubt, check your usage. If you are not certain of the word or the form of the word you are using, look it up in the dictionary. There are many words that are commonly confused, but they are very simple to check.

6. Keep Your Writing Gender-Neutral

The term **gender-neutral writing** refers to writing that avoids making unjustified assumptions about the gender of the person it describes. For example, writers have traditionally used the pronoun *he* to refer to an anonymous or generic person ("if a writer wants to be successful, *he* needs to understand grammar"). But times have changed. These days, the readers of your work, as well as the people you are writing about, are likely to be of both genders equally. It's in your best interest to make your reader feel included by your choice of words, so you should strive for gender-neutral writing at all times.

This doesn't mean that you have to butcher your writing. At most it will mean a little extra work, but in return you will reduce the risk of alienating your readers with language that could be interpreted as chauvinistic or outmoded. And the extra time you put into crafting your sentences carefully will probably make your writing more precise and easier to read.

Finally, you should use gender-neutral language because it follows our golden rule: avoid trouble. If a sentence could be misinterpreted, find another way to write it. The following is a quick guide for writing in a gender-neutral fashion.

The Obvious Stuff: Nouns

Whenever possible, avoid using generic terms based on the word "man."

Not Preferred	Preferred
man	human, personality
mankind	humanity, people, human beings
man-made	manufactured, synthetic, artificial
man-hours	work-hours, staff-hours

All I need to complete this job are a few good people.

Not: All I need to complete this job are a few good men.

Also, use the neutral form of job titles.

Not Preferred	Preferred
mailman	letter carrier
congressman	representative
policeman	police officer
fireman	firefighter
steward/stewardess	flight attendant
chairman	chairperson, coordinator

To protest this law, write to your congressional representative.

Not: To protest this law, write to your congressman.

The Harder Stuff: Pronouns and Possessives

The trickier part of gender-neutral writing is learning how to deal with pronouns. Here are some ways you can write your sentences to avoid these pitfalls.

1. Use the plural *they* or *them.*

   Because there is no gender-neutral singular pronoun in English, use the plural pronouns *they* and *them* to refer to people in general. The solution is to put everything in plural form.

   Yes: *Students* should solve *their* own *problems.*

   No: Every student should solve *his* own problem.

2. Replace the possessive with *a, an,* or *the.*

   Often there's no reason to use *his*—you can simply replace it with *a* or *the.*

   Yes: Give each candidate *the* exam upon arrival.

   No: Give each candidate *his* exam as soon as he arrives.

3. Eliminate the pronoun or possessive.

   In some cases, you can simply remove the pronoun or possessive, and the sentence will still be perfectly readable.

   Yes: Anyone who wants an ice cream should bring three dollars to class on Monday.

   No: Anyone who wants an ice cream should bring *his* three dollars to class on Monday.

4. Replace *he* and *him* with *he or she* and *his* with *his or her.*

   Yes: Each student should consult *his or her* advisor before registering.

   No: Each student should consult *his* advisor before registering.

   Another way to fix this sentence would be to follow #2:

   Each student should consult *an* advisor before registering.

5. Replace *he/him* with *you/your* or *one/one's* or another neutral noun.

> **Yes:** If *you* want to prevent confusion, *you* should avoid using *he* except when referring to a male.

> **No:** If a writer wants to prevent confusion, *he* should avoid using the word *he,* unless *he* is referring to a male.

If *one* wants to prevent confusion, *one* should avoid using the word *he* except when referring to a male. Also to prevent confusion, *writers* should avoid using the word *he* except when referring to a male.

7. Choose the Right Point of View

Avoid "I" in Academic Writing

Before you write, decide from what point of view you will write. This means you need to decide whether you want to refer to yourself in the first person singular, "I," as you would do in a personal essay. Alternatively, you may be writing about something from which you want to maintain a certain emotional distance—you may be writing an academic paper describing experiments you don't entirely approve of. Whatever the case may be, avoiding the first person "I" or "we" allows you to describe without necessarily putting your opinions in where they are not asked for. Most academic papers and exams are better written with no reference to the "I" author.

Use "I" in Personal Writing

Using the first person can make a writer appear more intimate with her reader, and make the writing more accessible. In a personal essay for a college or graduate school, the use of the first person "I" is expected and acceptable.

Use "You" With Caution

Directly addressing the reader is a dicey business, only to be attempted if you are sure it is both necessary and helpful to what you are writing. It is advisable if you are writing a how-to book, as we are doing here. In any other type of writing, avoid the use of the word "you." The easiest way to do this is to leave "you" understood. Here's an example:

Picture two men standing on the side of the road.

It is clear the author wants *you* the reader to picture the two men, but he avoids saying "you." The other, more formal way of avoiding "you" is to use "one," as in, "One never knows what one has missed until the moment has passed." It does sound stiff, but it can be useful, particularly in academic prose in which you should *never* use "you."

Be Consistent

Whatever point of view you select, stick with it throughout your piece. "We think it is important that I be consistent when she writes this book." See how inconsistency can throw you off? The less opportunity the reader has to be confused or befuddled, the better off the writer is.

8. Beware of Your Verbal Crutch

Most people have a word that they use as a catch-all for a variety of meanings. These words have their uses, but you should understand what your particular crutch means to you, whether it is "weird" or "like" or "whatever." You can then search it out in your writing and clarify your meaning by examining where it appears and substituting the word you really mean. If you cannot identify your personal verbal tic, get a second opinion by asking a friend or family member. Most likely they will know immediately.

9. Use Words Correctly

"He really weirded me out with that peanut butter pizza." Aside from the myriad of other faults in the preceding sentence, the word "weird" is used as a verb. "Weird" is *not* a verb; it is an adjective. There are enough words in the English language for you to express your meaning without resorting to this type of incorrect usage. For formal writing, try this instead:

> *I was horrified and disgusted by his peanut butter pizza.*

10. Use the Verb You Intend

When your verbs start to become dramatic, beware. The drama of your prose should come from your thoughts, not from melodramatic words. If you want to say someone walked into the street and asked someone for directions, by all means say so. For instance, you probably want to avoid, "He leapt off the curb and begged for help." In most cases, the more reserved your words, the more creative your writing.

11. Don't Use *Don't*

We know, we know, it isn't fair. If we can use contractions, how come you can't? Well, when writing something formal and academic, you must try to do what your instructor wants you to do. And the rule is, *avoid using contractions in academic writing.* As stilted as it may sound, use "do not" instead of "don't," and so on, unless you are writing something very informal that is meant to be conversational.

12. Keep Punctuation Simple (and Correct)

Let's eat Aunt Edna!
Let's eat, Aunt Edna!

Proper punctuation is indispensable to good writing. If the example above is any indication, commas can save lives. Look back to Chapter 2 for a review of the basic rules, or check out *Grammar Smart* for a more in-depth review. However, you should take care to avoid excessive punctuation. The powerful effect of your writing should come from the words you use, not from a series of exclamation points, dashes, or question marks.

Sentences

The sentence is the primary unit of grammar. Sentence structure is malleable—bendable, if you will. With proper punctuation and diction (word choice), syntax (sentence structure) can be changed to fit the needs of your audience. The way you'd write to a group of school children is far different from how you'd write to adults. You can always cover the same concepts, but the delivery of the subject matter is crucial to audience understanding.

Good sentences communicate a point clearly. When writing a sentence, it is helpful to ask yourself, "Does it say exactly what I mean?" Form what you want to say in your head, and then write that down. If your meaning is obscured, your sentence needs to be reworked. Often, the best writing is the simplest. So keep it simple.

The following guidelines will help you achieve greater clarity in your writing, but do not expect to write perfect sentences every time. Good writing also requires editing, revising, and rewriting, which we'll cover in the next chapter.

1. Vary Sentence Structure and Style

Sentences can start with their subjects, as this one just did. Or they can start with conjunctions, like this sentence. Using the same structure, sentence after sentence, can give your prose a droning, repetitive quality. So change it up every so often; your writing should be a mix of short and compound sentences.

2. Maintain Reasonable Expectations of Your Sentences

Most sentences convey one or two images. Don't overload your sentence with a freight too heavy for it to bear by adding comma after comma and phrase after phrase. You can always extend your metaphor or story or paragraph by adding sentences. Long sentences are difficult to control, so stick to manageable lengths. It is also easier to identify and repair flaws in shorter sentences.

> *I want to go to college and become more educated, because education is very important, and the economy is calling for people who have rigorous scholastic training.* Too much.

> *I want to go to college to become more educated. Education is very important, and the economy is calling for people with rigorous scholastic training.* Better.

3. Use the Active Voice

I bought a bagel.

or

A bagel was bought by me.

The first sentence is in the active voice, and the second is in passive voice. Whenever possible, use the active voice. The active voice is more concise, cogent, and appealing than passive; overall, it is simply more effective.

4. Use Humor with Caution

While many types of writing can often benefit from humor, a humorous tone is difficult to master. When you write, you can't rely on timing or inflection as you do when speaking; therefore, your sentences need to be carefully crafted in order to convey the correct tone. One way to check tone is to read aloud what you have written, using as little vocal inflection as possible. Is it still funny? If so, good work! If not, it's best to rework it or cut it altogether.

5. Include the Right Amount of Description

Description is an incredibly helpful tool in writing. It allows the writer to show more clearly what he or she intended.

For example, Nick included the following sentence in an essay on his college application. He is describing his employment in an effort to communicate to the admissions officer that because of his particular job, he has experience that will make him an outstanding candidate. Here is the sentence:

I work.

As the reader of this sentence, do you clearly understand what Nick is trying to communicate? Not really, and neither would the admissions counselor. How about:

> I work at the ice cream parlor.

Now you know more about Nick because he has altered his sentence to express more specifically what he is trying to communicate. Even so, if this is to be his introductory sentence, a sentence that includes more information may be appropriate:

> I work at the ice cream parlor near my house, and my job has taught me much about my neighbors.

But beware, while clear communication is essential, over-describing by tacking on description after description will muddy the prose and render the focus of the sentence unclear. For example:

> I work at the ice cream parlor near my house, which is in a low grey building made of old crumbling cinder block piled high and ominous against the mostly grey skies you find in Boston in November, and my job has taught me much about my neighbors.

Nick may walk away from that sentence patting himself on the back for his moving and descriptive turns of phrase, but as the reader, you get an entirely different message from the previous sentence. Too much description ends up weakening the entire sentence. Does he enjoy his work? Is that the point? Or is the ice cream parlor a depressing place? Or is his house? Unless you intend to use contradictions to enhance a sentence's meaning, avoid them.

6. Understand Metaphor, But Use It Sparingly

"Once at least in the life of every human, whether he be brute or trembling daffodil, comes a moment of complete gastronomic satisfaction."

—M.F.K. Fisher

A **metaphor** is a word or image used to describe something not like itself. Take the quote above, for example. *A human is a trembling daffodil.*

A metaphor is one of the most effective weapons in your arsenal. "A weapon?" you say. Ah, we were speaking metaphorically. Equating a word such as "weapon" to another is using metaphor. "That test was a piece of cake" is another metaphor. An extended metaphor lasts beyond the one image and can go on for sentences, or even paragraphs.

Extended metaphors are a difficult enterprise and are probably best avoided until you are more comfortable. Don't use a metaphor unless you feel that the thing you are describing could be better described in no other way. Otherwise, you will end up writing something like, "The car was a tiger running over the plains in the jungle," when it would have been far clearer to just write what you probably meant: "The car was fast and sleek."

Also avoid mixing metaphors. A mixed metaphor starts out with one image and ends with another: "That test was a piece of cake and it was smooth sailing all the way." The reader is left wondering whether the test is the cake or the water. You don't want to confuse your audience.

7. Understand Simile, But Use It Sparingly

> "As alarming as the Gaines-burgers were, their soy-meal began to seem like an old friend when the time came to try some canned dog foods."
>
> —Ann Hodgman

The sentence above refers to soy-meal seeming like an old friend, a perfect example of simile. A **simile** resembles a metaphor, but it uses the words *like* or *as*. Like other descriptive methods, simile should only be used when necessary to your sentence.

8. Create Images with Your Writing

> "Viewed from a suitable height, the aggregating clusters of medical scientists in the bright sunlight of the boardwalk at Atlantic City, swarmed there from everywhere for the annual meetings, have the look of assemblages of social insects."
>
> —Lewis Thomas

Good writing is clear writing. One of the great ways to make writing clear is to provide a vivid mental image for the reader to "see." The better you can set the scene, the easier it will be for the reader to follow you.

9. Ask Rhetorical Questions

"Where have all the thighs gone? Where are the
thighs of yesteryear? This is not exactly a litany
raised by many, but the heartfelt concern of a
few. In recent memory I do not believe that I have
entered a restaurant where thighs are allowed
to stand alone proudly by themselves. I mean
chicken thighs, though duck and turkey thighs are
also lonely and neglected."

—Jim Harrison

A rhetorical question is a question designed to stir up thought, and is not necessarily intended to be answered.

What is the use of a rhetorical question? Well, it can help you get your reader thinking about what is going through your mind. It can also help the reader to ask the question of himself, the question to which you will then thoughtfully provide the answer. Like other writing techniques, use rhetorical questions purposefully. Do not overuse them.

10. Know When to Use a Quotation

Have you noticed the quotations sprinkled throughout this chapter? Quotations can be helpful when you want to emphasize a certain point or further engage your reader. Just be careful not to overdo it. There should always be more of your writing in a paper than anyone else's. Don't quote for the sake of quoting; quote because someone has said something integral to your topic or point, and has said it far better than you can.

11. Follow Grammatical Conventions

That is, follow the rules of grammar. Don't think of grammatical conventions as limitations; think of them as a helpful guide to clearer, more effective communication. Continue to review Chapter 2 as you write.

Paragraphs

Once you have sentences, you can form paragraphs. Generally, each paragraph expresses a separate thought or idea. Paragraphs make reading easier, like cutting a steak into pieces to eat it, rather than trying to cram the whole thing into your mouth. Bear that image in mind both when you write and when you revise.

Paragraphs can be set off by indentation or by double-spacing. Either is acceptable, though indentation is the standard in most prose, and double-spacing is generally relegated to letter formats.

Starting a new paragraph requires a transition. Arrange your paragraphs so each one leads logically and seamlessly to the next. If you are going to start an entirely new thought that is not clearly connected to the previous paragraph, you may want to both indent and double-space, or start a new chapter if that sort of division is appropriate.

A Few Words About Modern Technology

To conclude this chapter, we would like to take some time to discuss these guidelines regarding word use and sentence construction as they apply to modes of communication most of us use every day: texting and social media.

Texting

Texting is writing, and the rules discussed in this chapter apply. The few extra seconds that it takes to type a proper English sentence often means the difference between presenting yourself well and presenting yourself, well—not so well. Here are some guidelines to follow:

1. Texts should never contain errors in grammar, diction, punctuation, or spelling. No matter how much of a rush you may be in, writing "your" instead of "you're" or texting a run-on sentence is wrong. Always check your texts before hitting the "send" button and fix any typos or errors created by autocorrect.

2. If you must use abbreviations and acronyms, use them sparingly. An occasional use of "textspeak" when chatting with friends or family is certainly fine, especially when used cleverly or to humorous effect. Too many, however, can suggest laziness, sloppiness, and poor writing ability. Texts sent in a professional context, or to recipients whom you don't know well, should not contain this type of shorthand.

3. Emojis and emoticons should be used to supplement words, not replace them. These symbols are fun to use and can enhance a joke or emphasize feelings. Unfortunately, however, they are often used as verbal crutches. Sending an electronic symbol when a written response is appropriate can be considered a "cop out." Taking the time to formulate a thoughtful reply, especially in awkward or delicate situations, is often what separates the good writer from the mediocre one.

4. Texts should be appropriate for the recipient. As with any piece of writing, you must consider your audience and alter your style accordingly. Group texts can be problematic when sent indiscriminately. Surely you would not use the same tone with your twelve-year-old nephew that you would with your boss, so be careful whom you include. If you must send texts to multiple recipients, consider writing several different messages of substance (one for family, another for business colleagues, etc.).

5. "Textspeak" has no place in formal writing. Slang terms, non-standard abbreviations and spellings, and emoticons have no place in any formal piece of writing. Unless you are quoting someone or otherwise indicate that a word or phrase deviates from proper English, do not use it. It's just that simple.

Social Media

Modern technology has created wonderful opportunities for us to communicate with people all over the globe in an instant and to exchange ideas on an unprecedented scale. Unfortunately, however, people who post publicly, whether on Facebook, Twitter, or other social media channel, do not always present themselves in the best light. The perceived anonymity of social media and the speed with which we can reply to one another leads to many exchanges that are not written with careful thought or attention to tone.

Before hitting "post," take a moment to review what you've written and make sure you are being clear, tactful and sensitive, and—ideally—grammatically correct. While you may be presenting yourself as an authority on a certain subject, you will undermine your own credibility if your response contains incorrect diction or grammatical errors. Further, is the post well-crafted, or simply written in haste as the result of strong emotion? More importantly, is it a respectful and dignified piece of writing? If you would be ashamed to have those words publicly attributed to you, don't hit "submit" or "post." Always remember that once you send an electronic communication, there is no taking it back. It is forever preserved in cyberspace.

Recommended Reading

The Staff of the Princeton Review, *Grammar Smart,* Penguin Random House.

Longman, *Roget's Thesaurus of Words and Phrases,* Penguin Random House.

William Strunk and E. B. White, *The Elements of Style,* Macmillan.

CHAPTER 4

Editing

The Editing Process

So you've written well-constructed sentences and strung them together to make coherent paragraphs, with transitions in between. At this point you have a rough draft in front of you. We hate to say it, but when you have a rough draft, you're still only about halfway there. Editing is the main work in writing excellent prose. It can be a tedious process eliminating words, sentences, even whole paragraphs, as well as moving text around and elaborating on certain points. But the results are well worth it.

When editing, try to read your work with an objective eye. You don't need to remind yourself how hard you worked on a particular paragraph or sentence; you need to decide what should be done with a particular paragraph or sentence *as it relates to the whole of what you are writing.* You are trying to refine the whole piece. All concerns other than the quality of that piece need to be ignored. You must stomp out that unhelpful part of your ego ("This metaphor is fantastic; even if it doesn't exactly work in this context, I need to keep it!"), and smother lazy urges ("Eh, it's good enough as is"). Make sure you allow yourself as much time as possible for this process. It is not the most pleasant for the majority of writers, and you may need to fortify yourself with frequent breaks for fuel in the form of snacks and non-literary entertainment. But when you're finished and have a polished final product in front of you, you'll be glad you put in the time and effort.

If you're editing a hard copy, your notations should be clear so that you know what you mean when you return to them later on. The notations on the next page are the proofreading marks that we will use in the editing exercises throughout this book. This does not mean you have to use these yourself; it means you can check back here when you are trying to figure out what a little squiggle might mean.

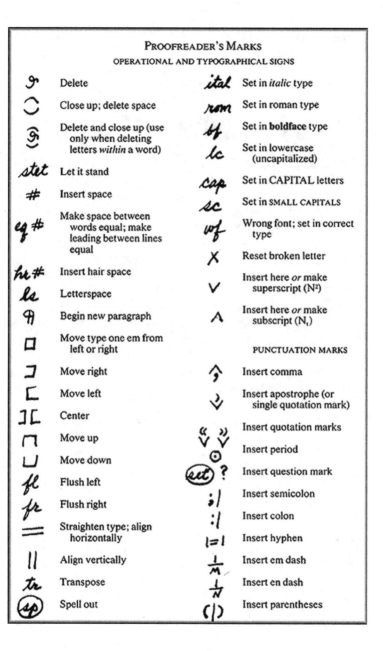

Editing usually takes place in at least three rounds. The first round should be focused on overall organization.

Round 1: Organization

Organization of a paper allows that paper to be read and understood logically. Much of editing lies not only in particular words or sentences but in whole paragraphs and sections of text. This is particularly true of longer pieces. On your first read-through of a longer piece, look for larger organizational issues.

Often your writing will seem particularly clear to you, when you are in fact missing important transitions or referring to a paragraph that doesn't come for another three pages. To avoid these problems, you need to spend some time at the rough draft stage of your paper. This is when you have everything you are going to include in the paper already written, but you haven't yet read through it for spelling or continuity, nor have you (most likely) added footnotes or other references. Before you go on to the fine-tuning stage, you need to make sure that your structure is sound.

First, read through the paper. Is it logical? Does everything seem to be in the proper order? Take notes as you read, indicating parts that seem unclear. Then divide your paper into sections. If your paper sets forth an opinion or argument, read through and separate it into the pieces of evidence that support your point. If your paper is a descriptive piece, separate it into the different facets of your subject.

One effective technique is to literally cut the paper with scissors. Compositions written in longhand should be photocopied, and works composed on the computer should be printed out as hard copies. Once you have separated your paper into pieces, spread them out and see if you can organize them into a more coherent whole. Experiment a bit here. Sometimes a paragraph that previously seemed dull or weak will take on a whole new life when it begins the body of a paper. Conversely, a paragraph that you had grown attached to can be exposed in this process as a nasty little parasite that is weakening the whole structure and coherence of your piece. Try many different setups, and keep a record of the ones that work best. It may be helpful here to make several copies and paste together your three best attempts at organization. You can also have other people read the paper at this stage, after having strung it together in a new way. Your friends or teachers can let you know whether you are being daring or just disorganized.

Round 1 Questions

- **Is this the logical way I would argue this point if I were talking to someone?**

   If you wouldn't talk this way on your best arguing day, there is probably a better way to organize your piece. Often ideas will come to you as you are writing, and you will include them as you think of them. This is all well and good, but it probably means that they are somewhat out of order. Once you have a rough draft, look at all the evidence and information you include. You can even put the subject of each paragraph on a note card, then move them around on the desk until they are well ordered. You may also want to read newspaper or magazine articles and essays to get examples of writing that flows logically and builds up to a main point, or thesis.

- **Do the paragraphs transition smoothly from one to the next?**

   This has much to do with the last and first sentences of paragraphs. Readers know intuitively that when a new paragraph begins, they should expect a somewhat new thought; but they also expect it to relate in some way to the thoughts just expressed. If there is no immediate connection, either create an entirely new section—not just a new paragraph—or write a transition sentence to begin the new paragraph. This transition sentence performs essentially the same function as a segue a comedian might make, like "So, speaking of kangaroos, I was talking to an Australian guy the other day. . . ." It allows the audience to follow your train of thought. You can still allow your reader to make some deductions, but don't force him to guess how things fit.

- **Are related paragraphs near each other?**

  If you refer to a dog named Gary in one paragraph, then refer to the dog again later as just "Gary," you need to ascertain that the reader knows to whom or to what you are referring. Be aware of this especially if you move paragraphs around in the editing process.

- **Does each paragraph explain itself well to the reader, or does it rely on additional, outside knowledge that should also be included?**

  In general, never assume knowledge on the part of the audience. This is true even if you're writing for a teacher or professor. For example, let's say in a history paper you write the following sentence: "After the war, there was a lot of trouble for everyone cleaning it up." Which war? Every subject in your paper should be explicitly introduced, defined, or explained.

Round 2: Style

When you have a structure you are comfortable with, you are ready for the next stage: editing for style.

You will probably notice some awkward sentences as you go through the reorganizing round. At this point, you will return and look for them mercilessly. If you are using pen and paper to compose, put these changes onto the pasted-together rough draft from your first round of edits. If you are using a computer, you can simply enter any corrections onto a saved version. It is probably helpful to print out that new version and put your edits on the hard copy. You can then enter them once you have gone through this second round.

When writing, try to get as much down as possible, but when editing, make sure that each piece is serving its appropriate function in its appropriate place.

Introductory sentences should be both engaging and concise. At the beginning of a paragraph, a paper, or an essay, you must try to open the door (yes, that's a metaphor) for your reader so she will look inside and want to enter. Whatever type of paper you are writing, you are creating a world that the reader will enter, even if only for a few sentences. Your opening sentence should orient your reader so she knows what you will be talking about and from what point of view.

Read each body paragraph carefully and determine whether your writing clearly communicates your logic. Scrutinize each sentence. Poke. Prod. If you find a sentence that doesn't work, rewrite it. If it still doesn't work after one or two rewrites, start a new sentence from scratch. Sometimes it is easier to create anew rather than work to fix something that is broken. You should also check for spelling, grammar, and punctuation here. Keep a dictionary and a copy of *The Chicago Manual of Style* on hand to check these fine points.

Round 2 Questions

- **Does this sentence convey its idea clearly?**

  When you were writing you knew what you meant, but will the reader know? "I felt as I always do when I hear Rachmaninoff," may mean you were frightened, exhilarated, or infuriated, but your reader will be unable to understand unless you open your private world of images to her. When you edit, think of this reader, and how each word, sentence, and paragraph would seem to her.

- **Does each sentence flow from the previous one?**

  Paragraphs should form coherent wholes. If there is too large a jump from sentence to sentence, the reader will become confused and lose the train of thought you have established.

- **Are any sentences unnecessary to the whole?**

  Extraneous sentences can bore a reader faster than anything else. In general, if within one paragraph you find two sentences that say the same thing, one of them can go. Of course, in certain circumstances repetition can be used for dramatic emphasis, and this is where you can again ask yourself, "Is this sentence necessary to the whole?" If not, strike it out.

- **Are any words unnecessary to the whole?**

  Redundancy is lethal to good style; avoid unnecessary words.

- **Is the point of view consistent?**

  Refer to the point of view section in the previous chapter. You should use only one point of view throughout a piece.

- **Is the tense consistent?**

  For clarity's sake, be consistent in your use of tenses.

- **Does this sentence say exactly what I mean?**

  You had a particular point you wanted to get across within each sentence you wrote. Does the sentence say what you meant? Check to see if a certain word could be fine-tuned to be more exact. "I wanted to take a walk before it got too dark" is not the same thing as, "I was afraid it would soon be too dark for me to walk safely." The first is matter-of-fact and slightly impatient, while the second implies a certain amount of trepidation, nervousness, and hesitation.

- **Is this sentence true?**

  This relates more to honesty in writing. Before you allow a sentence like, "The lightning flashed and a tree shuddered next to me, but I was not afraid," make sure that it is either literally true, or a very well-planned bit of misinformation, leading to humor or the like.

- **Is there a variety of sentence structure in this paragraph?**

  While a certain amount of sentence structure repetition can lend your writing a particular rhythm, the same sentence structure over and over will cause your readers to feel frustrated. If you see five sentences in a row beginning the same way, with "if" or an *–ing* word, see if you can transform a few of them.

- **Is each pronoun in this sentence necessary?**

  We are all subject to the modern-day plague of unnecessary pronouns. Chief among the culprits are "that," "which," and "it." When you see any one of this unholy trio, try the sentence without it. Does it still work? If so, eliminate the pronoun.

- **Does each pronoun refer to something the reader can understand?**

  You may find sentences that seem perfectly intelligible but have a mysterious floating pronoun. For example: *It is very difficult to understand why there is violence in this world.* The first "it" has no clear reference, and "this" preceding "world" makes it seem as though the writer has had some experience in other worlds, as does bringing up "the world" at all. *The existence of violence is incomprehensible* is a more concise way of expressing the same idea.

- **Is the sentence grammatically correct?**

  Take no chances here. If you are unsure, look it up. While you can amend spelling mistakes, typos, and punctuation in the last round of editing (though you will have caught most mistakes by then), grammatical errors often demand a reconstruction of the sentence. This reconstruction is too messy to appear on the final version of a paper, so attend to it now.

- **Do I avoid the passive voice?**

  That sounds much better than, "Has the passive voice been avoided by me?" doesn't it? When possible, sentences should be in the active voice. If you have a long, unruly, or dragging sentence, passive voice may well be the problem.

- **Does my verbal crutch appear anywhere?**

  A verbal crutch is a phrase or expression we use while speaking, sometimes to emphasize something or to (subconsciously) give ourselves more time to think. But often these crutches are used merely because they have become somehow embedded in our brains, and one result is that they turn up in our writing, too. Common verbal crutches include *actually, basically, honestly, literally, weird,* and *for the record.* If you know your verbal crutch, use the search-and-replace feature on your computer to search the document for its use. If you're not aware of your crutch or are working on a hard copy, just be vigilant. Read your piece carefully and circle any phrases that are used multiple times to the point that they become distracting and meaningless.

- **Do I have clichéd images?**

  Dark as night, bright like the sun, like a pack of vicious animals, on and on the cliché march goes. A cliché is an image that has been used so much and so often that it has actually been worn out. Readers are so used to seeing clichés that whatever power the image or saying once had is dismissed by the reader. Comb your writing for clichés. Whenever you see a phrase you recognize as overly familiar, strike it out.

- **Have I gone crazy with adverbs, adjectives, and other description?**

  Adverbs, along with most forms of description, should be used sparingly. Description should suggest, not give every detail. Don't overwhelm the reader.

- **Do I sound like myself?**

  Yes, you should sound like yourself. Don't try to seem more "writerly" or literary, as you will probably come off as trying too hard, or your meaning will get lost in a sea of complexity and words you found in the thesaurus. Your writing is a representation of you, so be true to who you are.

- **Is there stylistic closure?**

  Closure ties together loose ends and allows readers to feel they have truly finished, instead of being cut off in some premature way. Most writing requires some sort of conclusion to provide closure. The length of your conclusion will usually depend on the length of your piece. Symmetry may serve as an effective stylistical tool in creating closure. If you begin your paper with an anecdote, ending with an anecdote can be beautifully symmetrical. This also works if you begin with a quotation, a theory, or a historical reference. Consistency of example allows you to give your readers a feeling of satisfaction when they have reached the end of your paper. No matter how you accomplish it, closure is why a conclusion is necessary to most writing.

Round 3: Proofread

Before you do this final read-through, you must incorporate your edits from Round 2. If you're using a computer, you can enter these in the saved document. If you're using a pen and paper, you should write another draft.

Proofreading is your opportunity to indulge that nitpicking tendency you have kept hidden from the world. Or, this may be your opportunity to develop that streak. In the third round, you are looking for any tiny errors that may be floating around in your almost perfect manuscript. You are checking things you have already checked, like spelling, punctuation, typos, indentations, numbering on pages, underlining or italicization of titles (italics are preferable if you have them), and capitalization of proper names. If you are writing on a computer, you have the benefit of the spell check, though a spell check cannot identify all errors. So be extra careful and proofread for spelling anyway. When it doubt, look it up. For points other than spelling, keep that copy of *The Chicago Manual of Style* or the *MLA Handbook* with you, and mercilessly check all fine points.

Editing Drill 1

The following paragraph is part of a research paper discussing commercial novels of the 1980s, and it has many organizational and stylistic problems. Edit the paragraph, identifying these problems and addressing the questions brought up in the editing rounds we just discussed. Feel free to look back at previous chapters. Also keep in mind that since this paragraph is part of a research paper, it should have an academic tone. When you are done, compare the edits you made with our edits on the following page to see how they differ. If our edits don't correspond exactly with yours, don't be alarmed. Everyone edits in a different way, and your own personal style will have much to do with the words you choose to leave in or take out. After you have compared the two, look at the final version in which all the edits have been made. Are they what you would have done?

Some of the foremost examples of the trash novels of the eighties are those written by Jackie Collins and Judith Krantz. These novels mention in tiny meticulous detail all the money and the merchandise that money can procure, that belongs to their usually female characters. Thus, money becomes a dream of the woman of the nineteen eighties. This is not to say that these role models were only about money. Not only the money but what many of these novelists almost equated with money; fabulous looks and torrid romances. In Scruples, the tons of money, excessive pulchritude, and boundless ambition of the main character only convince you further of my point: so-called trash novels are attempts by women, for women, to cast themselves into a more positive fantasy than the one offered by other media, namely television and films of the same time.

Our Version, With Edits

most popular

unnecessary

passive voice instead of active

Some of the ~~foremost~~ examples of the trash novels of the eighties are those written by Jackie Collins and Judith

redundant

wrong word, maybe "describe"

Krantz. These novels mention in tiny meticulous detail ~~all~~ the money and the merchandise that money can

repeating word—also, does not make sense. rewrite sentence

"money" repeated too many times

procure, that belongs to their usually female characters. Thus, money becomes a dream of the woman of the nineteen eighties. This is not to say that these role models were only about money. Not only the money but what many

book? why no italics or author?

of ~~these novelists~~ almost equated with money; fabulous looks and torrid romances. In Scruples the tons of money

too casual

no need for fancy word, "beauty" okay

excessive pulchritude and boundless ambition of the main character only convince you further of my point: so-

not a full sentence

academic paper, no "you" or "me"

whole last sentence is main point—belongs at beginning

called trash novels are attempts by women, for women, to cast themselves into a more positive fantasy than the one offered by other media, namely television and films of the same time.

unnecessary

unnecessary

Final Version

The so-called trash novels of the eighties are attempts by women, for women, to cast themselves in more positive fantasy roles than those offered by other media. Jackie Collins and Judith Krantz wrote some of the most popular trash novels, which describe in meticulous detail the sumptuous financial situations of their heroines. Thus, these novels present financial stability as a dream of the woman of the 1980s. This is not to say that these role models were strictly mercenary. In these novels not only money, but what many of the novelists almost always equated with money—fabulous looks and torrid romances—represent the fantasies of women of the eighties. In *Scruples,* a novel by Judith Krantz, the money, beauty, and boundless ambition of the main character further demonstrate this point.

Editing Drill 2

The following is a personal essay in response to this question:

> Please provide us with a one-page summary of personal and family background. Include information on where you grew up, parents' occupations, any siblings, and perhaps a highlight or special memory of your youth.

Edit the essay for organization and style. Keep in mind the that this is a personal essay, and thus aims for a conversational tone. Then, review the edited version and compare our edits with your own. While you should not worry if your edits do not match exactly, do try to determine the differences in the edits. When you are done comparing the two drafts, look to the final version to see how the edits were accommodated.

My early life growing up in Powdonque, a sleepy New England town of about a thousand residents, was largely uneventful. I lived comfortably, but not really feeling too contented, with my parents and two younger brothers in an old gray house on the outskirts of a nice fishing community. My mother and father were both doctors who shared a medical practice and served as the town's principal physicians. While I had a lot of respect for my parents' profession, as did the rest of the world, for as long as I could remember I had dreamed of being a rock star. By the summer of my fourteenth birthday I had become thoroughly disdainful of small-town life. I spent my days in our family's garage drumming with my band, "The Weevils," that had been formed by me and three of my buddies—John, Paul, and George. When we weren't practicing together we would talk about all the exciting and thrilling places we would see when we inevitably embarked upon our first world tour. One hot Tuesday during the dog days of summer the heat in the garage was so oppressive that the four of us headed down to the lake for a swim. There we encountered an old rickety rope swing that, in our adolescent judgment, presented an irresistible opportunity for some raucous fun.

I was the first to soar across the lake and triumphantly plunge down into the cool water. John and George successfully followed suit, which lulled poor Paul into what would soon prove to be false sense of security. He had not yet even made it out a few yards when the swing broke and he plummeted to the ground, bumping his head on a boulder and losing consciousness. All was quiet for a minute or two while the three of us absorbed the surreal occurrence that had just transformed a lazy summer day into a calamity. The silence was rudely shattered as John started darting back and forth aimlessly, shrieking and shouting a long series of expletives. George admonished John for his hysteria, ordered him to compose himself, then ran toward the unconscious Paul. George began barking out medical directives: "Pour water on him and shake him hard until he wakes up!" "Stick something in his mouth so he doesn't swallow his tongue!" "Oh, jeez—if his head keeps bleeding like that, we'll have to make a tourniquet and put it around his neck!" At that moment an inexplicable sense of calm came over me and I took charge of the chaotic scene. I told John to run to the Johnsons' house and call 911, then told George to help me administer first aid to Paul. My parents had literally told me a million times about what to do in such a crisis; I heard their voices in my mind as I checked Paul's pulse, applied pressure to the wounds until the bleeding stopped, and was informing the paramedics of what little I knew of Paul's medical history. Paul made a full recovery, and the incident at the lake was soon reduced to an amusing anecdote among friends.

In the following years I still dreamed of becoming a rock star, but slowly the daily jam sessions in the garage were replaced by afternoons spent at my parents' clinic where I would help run the office after school and, whenever possible, observe my parents as they treated patients. Paul's accident had been an important event for me, although it took me many years to realize it. As I now apply to medical schools I can't imagine anything else that I would rather do with my life than practice medicine in my home town. I still want to be a rock star of sorts: a rock star just like my parents. Then there will be the names of three doctors, not two doctors, on the door of the Powdonque Family Medical Practice.

Our Version, With Edits

Why is this mentioned?

My early life growing up in Powdonque, a sleepy New England town of about a thousand residents, was largely uneventful. I lived comfortably, but not really feeling too contented, with my parents and two younger brothers in (an old gray house) on the outskirts of a (nice) fishing community. My mother and father were both doctors who shared a medical practice and served as the town's prin- cipal physicians. While I had (a lot of) respect for my par- ents' profession, as did (the rest of the world) for as long as I could remember I had dreamed of being a rock star. By the summer of my fourteenth birthday, I had become thoroughly disdainful of small-town life. I spent my days in our family's garage drumming with my band, "The Weevils," (that had been formed by) me and three of my buddies—John, Paul, and George. When we weren't prac- ticing, ~~together~~ we would talk about all the ~~exiting and thrilling~~ places we would see when we inevitably embarked upon our first world tour. One (hot) Tuesday during the dog days of summer the heat in the garage was so oppres- sive that the four of us headed down to the lake for a swim. There we encountered an old rickety rope swing that, in our adolescent judgment, presented an irresistible oppor- tunity for some raucous fun.

Nice in what way? Be more descriptive.

too informal; rephrase

perbolic

ssive ce

redundant

redundant

Use a more descriptive word

ché

These last two sentences should be part of the second paragraph (they discuss the incident with Paul).

I was the first to soar across the lake and triumphantly
plunge ~~down~~ [unnecessary] into the cool water. John and George suc- [wordy and awkward; rephrase] cessfully followed suit, which lulled poor Paul into what would soon prove to be false sense of security. He had not [This suggests a very long period of inaction] yet even made it out a few yards when the swing broke and he plummeted to the ground, bumping his head on a boulder and losing consciousness. All was quiet for (a minute or two) while the three of us absorbed the surreal occurrence that had just transformed a lazy summer day into a calamity. The silence was rudely shattered as John started darting back and forth aimlessly, shrieking and shouting a long series of expletives. George admonished John for his hysteria, ordered him to compose himself, then ran toward the unconscious Paul. George began barking out medical directives: "Pour water on him and shake him hard until he wakes up!" "Stick something in his mouth so he doesn't swallow his tongue!" "Oh, jeez—if his head keeps bleeding like that, we'll have to make a tourniquet and put it around his neck!" At that moment, an inexplicable sense of calm came over me and I took charge of the chaotic scene. I told John to run to the Johnsons' house and [no need to specify here] call 911, then told George to help me administer first aid [misuse of the word "literally"] (to Paul.) My parents had (literally) told me a million times about what to do in such a crisis; I heard their voices in my mind as I checked Paul's pulse, applied pressure to the wounds until the bleeding stopped, and (was informing) the

[the verbs in this list should be in parallel form]

paramedics of what little I knew of Paul's medical history. Paul made a full recovery, and the incident at the lake was soon reduced to an amusing anecdote among friends.

In the following years, I still dreamed of becoming a rock star, but slowly the daily jam sessions in the garage were replaced by afternoons spent at my parents' clinic where I would help run the office after school and, whenever possible, observe my parents as they treated patients. Paul's accident had been an important event for me, although it took me many years to realize it. As I now apply to medical schools, I can't imagine anything else that I would rather do with my life than practice medicine in my home town. I still want to be a rock star of sorts: a rock star just like my parents. Then there will be the names of three doctors, not two doctors on the door of the Powdonque Family Medical Practice.

Separate this long sentence into two sentences.

Use a more powerful word here.

redundant

Final Version

My early life growing up in Powdonque, a sleepy New England town of about a thousand residents, was largely uneventful. I lived comfortably, if discontentedly, with my parents and two younger brothers on the outskirts of a quaint fishing community. My mother and father were doctors who shared a medical practice and served as the town's principal physicians. While I had a healthy respect for my parents' profession, as did the rest of the community, for as long as I could remember I had dreamed of being a rock star. By the summer of my fourteenth birthday I had become thoroughly disdainful of small-town life. I spent my days in our family's garage drumming with my band, The Weevils," that I had formed with three of my buddies—John, Paul, and George. When we weren't practicing we would talk about all the exciting places we would see when we inevitably embarked upon our first world tour.

One sweltering August Tuesday the heat in the garage was so oppressive that the four of us headed down to the lake for a swim. There we encountered an old rickety rope swing that, in our adolescent judgment, presented an irresistible opportunity for some raucous fun. I was the first to soar across the lake and triumphantly plunge into the cool water. John and George successfully followed suit, which lulled poor Paul into what would soon prove to be false sense of security. He had barely made it out a few yards when the swing broke and he plummeted to the ground, striking his head on a boulder and losing consciousness. All was quiet for a moment while the three of us absorbed the surreal occurrence that had just transformed a lazy summer day into a calamity. The silence was rudely shattered as John started darting back and forth aimlessly, shrieking and shouting a long series of expletives. George admonished John for his hysteria, ordered him to compose himself, then ran toward the unconscious Paul. George began barking out medical directives: "Pour water on him and shake him hard until he wakes up!" "Stick something in his mouth so he doesn't swallow his tongue!" "Oh, jeez—if his head keeps bleeding like that, we'll have to make a tourniquet and put it around his neck!" At that moment an inexplicable sense of calm came over me and I took charge of the chaotic scene. I told John to run to the Johnsons' house and call 911, then told George to help me administer first aid. My parents had so often instructed me about what to do in such a crisis; I heard their voices in my mind as I checked Paul's pulse, applied pressure to the wounds until the bleeding stopped, and informed the paramedics of what little I knew of Paul's medical history. Paul made a full recovery, and the incident at the lake was soon reduced to an amusing anecdote among friends.

In the following years I still dreamed of becoming a rock star, but slowly the daily jam sessions in the garage were replaced by afternoons spent at my parents' clinic. I would help run the office after school and, whenever possible, observe my parents as they treated patients. Paul's accident had been a watershed moment for me, although it took me many years to realize it. As I now apply to medical schools I can't imagine anything else that I would rather do with my life than practice medicine in my hometown. I still want to be a rock star of sorts: a rock star just like my parents. Then there will be the names of three doctors, not two, on the door of the Powdonque Family Medical Practice.

Finally . . .

There are some people who benefit from more than three drafts of a paper. You must become accustomed to your own ways of writing to determine if you are one of these people. Every writer is unique, and eventually you will develop your own personal style of editing.

Recommended Reading

The Chicago Manual of Style, The University of Chicago Press.

William Strunk and E. B. White, *The Elements of Style,* Macmillan.

Miss Thistlebottom's Hobgoblins, *The Careful Writer's Guide to the Taboos, Bugbears, and Outmoded Rules of English Usage,* Farrar, Straus, and Giroux.

CHAPTER 5

Personal Essays

The Art of the Personal Essay

A college or graduate school may ask you to write a personal essay to find out more about who you are and how you think. The essay might ask one of those horrifyingly vague questions like, "Tell us more about yourself in the space provided," or, "Describe an experience that has shaped you." Although writing a personal essay can seem challenging or intimidating, the great thing about them is that they give you the opportunity to write about something that you know a lot about: yourself. The truth is most people take a healthy interest in what they do; otherwise, why would they do it? And generally, people write best when they are discussing something that interests them.

Format

The general structure of a personal essay will vary slightly with its proposed length, but will follow this basic form: introduction, three examples, conclusion.

- **Introduction:** Your introduction will state the point you wish to make and set up the way you will make your point. This means that before you start writing your introduction, you must know what you intend to say.

- **Examples:** Each of these should be a separate paragraph and provide clear tangible evidence to support your introductory claim. For instance, if you start out saying, "I realized in the middle of last summer that I enjoy fishing," your examples must demonstrate this with some clarity: "In July I went to visit my mother in Alaska where we fished for halibut in the inland waterway." Also remember that you can have a strong point of view in a personal essay. If you enjoy fishing and believe this says something about you, don't be afraid to express your enjoyment through description. "The salt smell and the stillness of the water thrilled us, and as the day wore on we were astonished to see whales surfacing and eagles skimming the waves, all before I felt the first exciting tug on my line." Your examples can bring up subtleties of the main point you posited in your introduction. They should fill in the main point as though the main point were an outline in a coloring book and the examples were the crayons used to color it in and make it vibrant and exciting for the viewer.

- **Conclusion:** The conclusion should basically restate, in different words, the main point you presented in the introduction. You may also use this last paragraph to tie in the examples you used through the middle of your essay. Because of this, your conclusion will usually resonate more than your introduction. If the introduction is the outline and the examples color it in, the conclusion gives your work of art its title, taking into account both its shape and its color.

Writing the Personal Essay: Nick

Step 1: Focus on What You Want to Say

"A writer should concern himself with whatever absorbs his fancy, stirs his heart, and unlimbers his typewriter."

—E. B. White

One of the most challenging aspects of a personal essay is its tight limitation on space; therefore, a focused thesis is key. This thesis should present you to your advantage. Applying to school is competitive, and you are responsible for the image you present. Your job is to enlighten the admissions committee about your wonderful qualities. No one else will do this for you. Since most personal essay questions are generalized and free-form, you may want to jot down a few things that are important to you and stew over them for a bit. Think about what you want to present to the admissions committee as your most winning character trait.

Nick is applying to a highly competitive university. Here is the essay prompt on the application.

> Please write an essay (250–500 words) about something of direct personal importance to you. Use this opportunity to give us a clearer sense of you as an individual.

Daunting enough? We think so.

Nick considers what he would like to say. He has moved around with his family because his father is in the Air Force, and they have transferred many times to and from bases, but he does not want to write about his rootlessness. He wonders, what has been occupying his mind when he spaces out in American history class? His favorite thing to do is to sit in his room and listen to music and space out. He thinks of unusual music from Yemen that he listened to recently—it inspired and shocked him. Why did it do that?

Step 2: Write Down Your Main Point

Writing down your main point does not necessarily mean that you will use the resulting sentence in your essay, only that this sentence will exist to focus you on the point you are trying to get across. Once you have your focus, every sentence in your essay will serve to sharpen that focus.

> Nick writes, "When I listened to that unfamiliar Yemeni music, I realized that people live and grow up anywhere in the world and that seems natural to them, just like my life seems natural to me. I think it's strange to live there, and they probably think it's strange to live in the U.S." He decides that writing about the way the music makes him feel, rather than the music itself, will be more helpful because he knows more about that, and it will show more about him.

Step 3: Write the Rough Draft

Once you have your main point, you know what your first paragraph will cover: an introduction of that main point. This can be done in a creative manner, and it should be told as a story when possible. Most people are interested in stories. The personal essay allows you to stray from the form of the academic paper; it allows you to express yourself with vibrancy, wit, and a more casual and narrative form than most other types of writing. The paragraphs following that first one amplify your main point and give clear examples. The conclusion restates the main point. Since you are writing a rough draft here, allow yourself to go over the recommended page limit if you feel like it. You can cut later; now is the time to get as much raw material on paper as you can. Experiment, gush, go on and on about your dog Charlie or whatever strikes your fancy. You can reorganize and refine later.

Step 4: Edit the Rough Draft

Now that you have gotten it all down on paper, it is time to edit. Take a look at the following drill.

Drill 1

Edit the following essay, focusing on making it clearer and more concise. Look for any awkward sentences, and note ways that Nick might be able to interest his readers. Also make sure that the main point is evident and supported throughout the piece. When you are done editing, look at our version on page 106.

One day this past November, when I came home from school, I was exhausted and dispirited. I thought of all the homework I had to do and the chores I had to finish. I remembered that it was only going to get colder and rainier. I had taken some music recordings out from the library for an assignment for my music appreciation class, and I decided that this assignment would be the easiest to begin. My teacher wanted us to select music of a culture we knew nothing about and to listen to it. I had chosen music from Yemen.

I lay down on my bed and turned on the music and shut my eyes. It is not that I have never listened to music before; I listen to it as much as anyone my age, on the radio in the car, at parties, with friends. For the next fifteen minutes I listened in a way that I have not listened before.

It is difficult for me to describe the way the music sounded. It was filled with twanging curving screeches, and warbling of old men. It was not beautiful in any way I have ever considered, and I would never put it on for background music at a party. But when I listened to it, I saw the world from which it came. Of course I will never really know unless I visit there whether what I imagined is really what Yemen is like. I saw sand and blue sky and children in robes. I thought of the children and I realized that there must be boys there like myself, seventeen years old and nearing the end of whatever they have for high school, and hearing this music as part of their daily life. I know western culture has permeated large sections of the world, but I thought of growing up there, or really growing up somewhere else, anywhere else. The world there is entirely different, and people exist there the same as they do here, and grow up and fight with their parents and move out and age and die. It amazed me.

I know I still have all the ethnocentrism of my culture, and I have lost a bit of the feeling that I had when listening to the music. But I remember knowing, just for a moment, how big the world is and how much there is to it, with every different person and every different country a separate specific part of the whole world.

Our Version, With Edits

Here are the edits we made. No two people edit the same way, so don't be alarmed if you would have chosen very different rewrites. Do pay attention to the redundancies and awkward sentences that we point out, as these are the types of things you should catch when you are editing your own writing.

already said

too many sentences begin with "I"

need a better transition between thoughts here

One day this past November, when I came home from school, I was exhausted and dispirited. I thought of all the homework I had to do and the chores I had to finish. I remembered that (it) was only going to get colder and rainier. I had taken some music recordings out from the library for an assignment for my music appreciation class, and I decided that this assignment would be the easiest to begin. My teacher wanted us to select music of a culture we knew nothing about and to listen to it. I had chosen music from Yemen.

what does "it" refer to?

suggest changing this; you don't want to seem lazy!

listen to

foreshadow with "expecting nothing"

change in thought and tone— new ¶

I lay down on my bed and turned on the music and then shut my eyes. It is not that I have never listened to music before; I listen to it as much as anyone my age, on the radio in the car, at parties, with friends. For the next fifteen minutes I listened in a way that I have not listened before.

then

unnecessary

maybe put in a "but" because this is in contrast

It is difficult for me to describe the way the music sounded. It was filled with twanging curving screeches, and warbling of old men. It was not beautiful in any way I

why "it"?

have ever considered, and I would never put it on for background music at a party. But when I listened to it, I saw *imagined I*
the world from which it came. Of course I will never really *they know*
this—make
know unless I visit there whether what I imagined is really *it one word*
what Yemen is like. I saw sand and blue sky and children *in previous*
sentence
in robes. I thought of the children and I realized that there *people*
must be boys there like myself, seventeen years old and *this is a*
main point!
nearing the end of whatever they have for high school, *put at end*
and hearing this music as part of their daily life. I know
western culture has permeated large sections of the world,
~~but I thought of growing up there, or really growing up~~
~~somewhere else, anywhere else.~~ The world there is entirely
different, and people exist there the same as they do here,
and grow up and fight with their parents and move out and
age and die. It amazed me.

why tell   I know I still have all the ethnocentrism of my cul-
them this
ture, and I have lost a bit of the feeling that I had when
listening to the music. But I remember ~~knowing~~ just for
a moment, how big the world is and how much there is to
it, ~~with every different person and every different country~~
~~a separate specific part of the whole world.~~

nonsense, needs a more   *too many "buts"—use "neverthe-*
personal ending   *less, that music made me know*

relate back to first ¶

Step 5: Write the Final Draft

Make the edits you found during Step 4 and polish it up. This final draft contains all the edits made in the revision process, as well as some new edits. It has the proper paragraph format and has been checked for spelling and other mistakes.

Read the following version of Nick's essay, which incorporates the suggested revisions and has been edited for length. Pay attention to how certain issues (such as awkward sentences) were fixed.

One day this past November, I came home from school exhausted and dispirited, thinking of all the homework to do and the chores to finish. November meant more cold and rain. I dragged myself to my room to begin my homework by listening to some music for an assignment for my music appreciation class. My teacher wanted us to select music of a culture we knew nothing about, and I had chosen music from Yemen. I sat down on my bed and turned on the music and shut my eyes, expecting nothing.

I listen to music often; I listen to it on the radio in the car, at parties, with friends. But for the next fifteen minutes, I listened in a way I had not listened before.

Describing the sound of the music is difficult. It was filled with twanging curving screeches and the warbling of old men. It was not beautiful in any way I have ever considered, and I would never put it on for background music at a party. But as I listened, I imagined that I saw the world from which it came. I saw sand and blue sky and children in robes. The world there is entirely different, yet people exist there the same as they do here. They grow up, fight with their parents, move out, age, and die. I was amazed. I realized that there must be boys there like myself, seventeen years old and nearing the end of whatever they have for high school, and hearing this music as part of their daily life. To them, growing up in Yemen is normal, and growing up in the United States is strange.

Hearing that music made me know, just for a moment, how big the world is and how much there is to it, of music, and cultures, and the people who make up both these things. It pulled me from the hole of my November and showed me the world, for an instant.

Writing the Personal Essay: Hanna

We recommend following the same format and steps when writing an essay for a graduate school application. Generally, the sorts of questions asked on grad school applications do not significantly differ from those asked on college applications; the main difference is the experience you have accrued by the time you apply to graduate school. Again, the goal is to produce a clear, organized piece of writing that presents the best version of yourself and demonstrates how you stand out.

Step 1: Focus on What You Want to Say

Hanna is applying to business schools, and the following question appears in one of the applications.

> Please provide us with a one-page summary of personal and family background. Include information on where you grew up, parents' occupations, any siblings, and perhaps a highlight or special memory of your youth.

Hanna thinks about her childhood and family: playing outside, going to school, bonding with her siblings. All of this matters, but what experiences shaped her the most? More to the point, what experiences might have brought her to this stage of her life in which she is applying to business school? Why is she going to business school anyway? That must be the focus of the application, and she wants to present herself in the most positive light possible to increase her chances for admission. What part of her childhood most influenced her decision to attend business school? She thinks of her Aunt Susan, who visited when she was eight: Aunt Susan, on her way to law school and very excited. Hmm.

Step 2: Write Down Your Main Point

Hanna writes, *When Aunt Susan visited she was happy for the first time ever and it made me happy to see her. I think she was happy because she had direction, and now I do too.* This way, she figures, she can answer the question posed, and present herself to the admissions staff as someone really serious about going to business school.

Step 3: Write the Rough Draft

Hanna thinks back to that special day when her Aunt Susan visited and writes down anything and everything that she can remember. She doesn't worry about writing perfect sentences. She doesn't worry about exact chronology. She gets her thoughts down on paper—that's it.

Step 4: Edit the Rough Draft

Edit Hanna's rough draft just as you edited Nick's essay a few pages back. Then check your edits against the version on the following page. The goal is to make the essay concise and interesting. Don't worry if your edits are not the exact same edits that appear on the following page. No two people edit the exact same way. But look for the differences, and try to analyze why the edits on the following page were chosen.

Drill 2

I grew up in Baltimore, Maryland, with both my parents and two sisters. My father was a baker, and my mother worked as a teacher's aide. Both my parents came from large families and there were always relatives of one side or another stopping by to visit. I remember when my mother's youngest sister, my Aunt Susan, came to visit us one August.

Aunt Susan was the sister my mother always worried about, and talked to my father about over dinner. She would say Susan was unfocused, she had no steady suitor, she was wandering around doing nothing with her life even though she'd had a college education, which not all of the siblings had had. Susan was one of my favorite Aunts. She was nearest my age and the wandering that my mother worried over seemed romantic and thrilling to me.

While we waited for her my mother said, "Susan has something big to tell us. Now I don't know what it is but we should all be very supportive because any decision Susan makes has to be for the better." When Susan came, we all adjourned to the kitchen table which was where all the announcements were made. Susan looked happier than I ever remember seeing her. "I've decided to go to law school," she said, "And I'm going to work for the ACLU when I get out. I'm going to help people."

I had never seen Aunt Susan sure of anything before, but it was clear she was sure now. She did go to law school, and while it was not easy along the way, she got a job with the ACLU, and she works there to this day.

Seeing Aunt Susan decide she wanted something, and then watching her go an get it was thrilling. She had always been a romantic if troubled figure. With her decision and determination, she was not only wonderful, but also strong and happy. I think of that night often, because I feel I have come to the same point in my life, and business school is the place I will find my fulfillment.

Our Version, With Edits

make one introductory sentence — I grew up in Baltimore, Maryland, with ~~both my parents~~ and two sisters. My father ∧was a baker, and my mother ∧worked as a teacher's aide. Both my parents came from large families and there were always relatives of one *unnecessary, already clear* side or another stopping by to visit. I remember when my mother's youngest sister, my Aunt Susan, came to visit us one August.

Aunt Susan was the sister my mother always worried about and ~~talked to~~ *discussed with* my father ~~about~~ over dinner. She would say Susan was unfocused (~~she had no steady suitor,~~ ~~she was~~ wandering around doing nothing with her life even *weird wording* though she'd had a college education, which not all of the *bad ending and need more about Aunt Susan* siblings had had. Susan was ~~one of~~ *too wishy-washy* my favorite Aunts. She was nearest my age, and the wandering that my mother worried over seemed romantic and thrilling to me.

unclear—say when: "the night before" While we waited for her my mother said, "Susan has *two separate thoughts* something big to tell us. Now I don't know what it is, but we should all be very supportive because any decision Susan makes has to be for the better." When Susan came, we all adjourned to the kitchen table (which was) where *unnecessary* all the announcements were made. Susan looked happier *more dramatic starting with "she said"* than I ever remember seeing her. "I've decided to go to law school," she said, "And I'm going to work for the ACLU when I get out. I'm going to help people."

tense — I had never seen Aunt Susan sure of anything before, but it was clear she was sure (now.) ¶ She did go to law school, and while it was not easy along the way, she got a job with the ACLU, and she works there (to this day.) —*cliché*

Seeing Aunt Susan decide she wanted something, and then watching her go an(d) get it *was thrilling*. She had *typo* always been a (romantic, if) troubled figure. With her decision and determination, she was not only wonderful, but also strong and happy. I think of that night often, because I feel I have come to the same point in my life, and business school is (the place) I will find my fulfillment.

where or how?

Step 5: Write the Final Draft

I grew up in Baltimore with my father, a baker, my mother, a teacher's aide, and my two sisters. There were always relatives of one side or another stopping by to visit. My mother's youngest sister, my Aunt Susan, came to visit us one August when I was twelve.

Aunt Susan was the sister my mother always worried about and discussed with my father over dinner. She would say Susan was unfocused, wandering around doing nothing with her life though she'd had a college education, something my mother lacked. Susan was lost. Susan was in trouble. Susan was my favorite aunt. She was nearest my age, and the wandering that my mother worried over seemed romantic and thrilling to me.

The night before Aunt Susan was to arrive, my mother said, "Susan has something big to tell us. Now I don't know what it is, but we should all be very supportive because any decision Susan makes has to be for the better." When Susan walked in, it was clear that something had changed. She was as fascinating as ever, with tales of her crazy, exciting life. But this time her stories revolved around a temporary job in a law office. I figured that the existence of Susan's job was her shocking announcement, big enough to account for the surprise my mother had referred to. But then Susan called us into the kitchen, where all family announcements were made. She looked happier than I had ever seen her. She said, "I've decided to go to law school, and when I'm finished I'm going to work for the ACLU. I'm going to help people."

I had never seen Aunt Susan sure of anything before, but she was clearly sure then.

Nothing in my life has made a greater impression on me than Aunt Susan's decision. While the law has never intrigued me as it did her, her desire, and her focus once she had decided what she wanted to do, thrills me still to think of it. She did go to law school, and while it was not easy along the way, she got a job with the ACLU, and she works there now.

I think of that night often, because I feel I have come to a similar point in my life, and business school is my avenue to fulfillment.

Specific Essay Questions

When you are given less leeway in your essay question—that is, when an application asks you to respond to a more directed question—what do you do? Some examples of more specific essay questions are:

If you could be a talk show host and you could have the opportunity to interview any three prominent persons living or deceased, whom would you choose, why, and what would you discuss?

Discuss an issue of personal, local, national, or international concern, and its importance to you.

Select a creative work: a novel, film, poem, musical piece, painting, or other work of art that has influenced the way you view the world and the way you view yourself. Discuss the work and its effect on you.

Highlight your academic accomplishments.

Tell us how a form of art or entertainment has affected you.

These essays follow the rules of all nonfiction writing. Be honest and write about a subject that has meaning for you.

If confronted with a question like the first one on the previous page, don't go after the big names—Einstein, Lincoln, Washington—without a very good reason for wanting to talk with them. Often a writer will invoke these names in the blind hope that some of their greatness will rub off on the writer. Not so. The schools that request these types of essays are not doing so because they want to see if you can identify what a great person is, they are doing it because they want to know more about you personally, and your individual way of seeing the world. Try to select people you would truly like to speak with, and your personality will shine through.

The other essay questions here ask you to present one particular facet of yourself, so focus on just one in your essay. If you are asked about your most important experience, describe one that illuminates your strengths. Qualities worth highlighting on a college or graduate school application: diligence, responsibility, honesty, tenacity, resilience in the face of difficulty, creativity (particularly in the case of finding solutions for problems), curiosity (both academic and otherwise). And as we have stressed over and over: be honest. Every human being in the world has some good qualities, and the only way to write this sort of essay well and cogently is to tell the truth. If you cannot identify any characteristics you think will impress an admissions committee, ask friends and other loved ones. They have that perfect blend of objectivity and affection. You may feel embarrassed writing about yourself in such a self-aggrandizing manner; just keep in mind that you were asked to do so.

School-Focused Questions

How will University X help further your career goals?

Discuss your reasons for wanting to attend Y University; how does it differ from other schools on your list?

When the focus of your essay needs to be on the institution and your reasons for applying there specifically, stay away from pure flattery. The admissions committee wants to determine whether you are informed about that particular institution and its programs. The key here is to do a bit of research. Find out what the university considers its best features; is it small with a terrific student-to-teacher ratio, or is it large with fabulous research facilities? Read everything you can find on the Internet to identify the university's strengths, and then figure out where these strengths intersect with your desires and write about that.

Common Personal Essay Pitfalls

Writing a Biography

Don't feel tied to chronology. You are asked to produce a personal essay because the asker wants to know something further about you. This does not necessarily mean that your essay must include a detailed biography. You can indicate more about yourself by discussing your thoughts on current events or morality or scientific ethics. You can tell a story about your life, but it does not necessarily have to be set as a straight biography beginning with the day you were born and detailing each event to the present. Stick to what really interests you and you'll have a more interesting essay.

Lacking Direction or a Main Point

A personal essay is not a mandate to list the events of your life. Before you start writing, have an idea of what you intend to say. You must have a main point. Your main point can be that you learned through many years of shopping for shoes that shopping was for you an opportunity to understand capitalism and our culture. Your main point can be that by watching the film *Bambi* you realized how transitory and powerful the idea of life on this earth is for you. Whatever you write about, you must have a point in mind. Simply listing the events in your life will lead you to write a journal entry, not an essay.

Misrepresenting Yourself

Most people fear that they are boring and that the admissions officer for whatever program they are applying to will certainly realize this and toss their application into the rejection pile. To make themselves stand apart, these folks think of the oddest thing they do and write about that. Before you run out and write your essay about your encounter with space aliens, remember our guideposts: clarity and honesty. If you don't really believe that eating fried fire ants in the desert was important for you, don't write about it. Not only will you misrepresent yourself, but you will also be writing about something you don't really care about, which leads to muddled, messy work. Your perspective makes an essay interesting, not the actual subject. While many phenomena are common, people are singular, and your particular experience and the angle from which you saw it can be duplicated by no one else. Therefore, that view, that particular perspective, is what you should aim to convey in your essay.

Getting Too Detailed

When you write a personal essay, you may get into territory most readers are not too familiar with: your family, your town, and so on. While it is necessary to introduce characters or settings with which your reader may be unfamiliar, "My friend Toby," or "The dump down the hill from my house," it is unhelpful to describe anything in greater detail than the essay really calls for. It is probably unnecessary to inform the reader of Toby's hair color unless you are writing an essay regarding a major hair-dyeing trauma you experienced.

Being Overly Dramatic

"The day I dyed my hair so I would look more like Toby was the most momentous day of my life." Think for a moment, is this really true? Or are you trying to get your reader interested by yelling, in effect, "Over here, over here! Big things!" When you reread your essay, be sure to check for words such as "ever," "never," and "the most." Allow your thoughts and ideas to be the drama of the moment. Remember, the reader is already reading the essay. By getting overly dramatic you make your writing seem desperate to be noticed, which is no more attractive in prose than it is in people.

Redundancy

People are tempted to begin sentences with, "I think," or "I believe." In a personal essay, this is bad form. If you are writing the essay, then anything you write is something you think, feel, or believe. To say so explicitly is redundant.

Excessive Informality

Just because you are writing about something personal is no reason for your prose to become casual or intimate. The tone of a personal essay can be more relaxed and informal, but do not let your writing become a mere record of a conversation. Your aim is clarity, so excessive folksiness is to be avoided. Your ideas will allow the reader to view you as you are, and the way to present them clearly is to write them clearly.

Boasting, Rambling, and Using Boilerplate Language

Self-confidence is a good thing, and there's a way to convey confidence without seeming narcissistic or overly self-congratulatory. It can be a fine line to walk sometimes, especially when the purpose of the essay is to promote yourself. Have an objective-minded teacher or brutally honest friend read the essay to ensure your tone is appropriate.

Avoid writing more than the required or requested number of words or pages. Writing pages and pages over the requested limit isn't just a blatant disregard for the essay parameters—it will also cause your reader to shut down altogether and probably put your essay aside. Next.

Finally, don't submit the same essay for multiple schools. Admissions officers can usually detect a boilerplate essay (vague statements are a giveaway!), so keep your essays specific. We understand that writing one solid essay is hard enough; how can you write two, three, or more additional essays? Trust us, we get it. But remember that you don't need to reinvent the wheel every time. Let that first essay be your template, and then tailor the language to the various schools to which you're applying.

Formatting and Using Citations in Your Personal Essay

- There is no set format for references in a personal essay. Many writers include mentions of their favorite authors, books, or other things that may have influenced them, but such references are listed in the essay and not given as part of any sort of bibliography.

- Be sure to follow the instructions regarding spacing, font, margins, and so on. If no specifics are given, double-space for easier reading.

- Indent your paragraphs; don't use an extra space.

- Titles are unnecessary in the personal essay. Unless you can think of a really great one, don't use a title.

In Conclusion. . .

The purpose of a personal essay is to share something about yourself. You must be honest and forthcoming, and write about something that matters to you. As long as you present a true passion of yours and check your work for the pitfalls described in this chapter, you can be sure your essay will have the impact and the originality required.

CHAPTER 6

Timed Writing

The Art of the Timed Essay

When given time to research, outline, and edit, one can write a serviceable term paper. (More on this in Chapter 7!) In an exam situation, however, when you're writing against the clock, how do you produce a clear, organized, and well-argued essay? Knowing how to approach any piece of timed writing is an essential skill for many standardized tests that feature an essay, such as the SAT. And this same skill can be applied to situations outside the classroom or testing center, such as when you are writing to hit a deadline at work.

The following format is recommended for essay tests, but you can also use it for any type of non-personal essay, including editorials, reviews, and creative nonfiction. See the recommended reading list at the end of the chapter for books that include this type of essay. Reading examples of a literary form can inspire you in your own writing.

Basic Template for Timed Essays

The basic format for timed essays or any non-personal essay includes an introduction, body, and conclusion.

Introduction

An introduction is a brief response to the question, consisting of a paragraph made up of just a few sentences. It is, essentially, how you would respond to the question if you weren't forced to write an entire page on the subject.

Body

The body of the essay includes in most cases three (sometimes more or fewer) paragraphs, with specific examples in support of the answer you present in your introduction.

Conclusion

The conclusion is a restatement of your introduction, with some notes on how the intervening examples clearly support your contention.

Writing the Timed Essay

Step 1: Research

The research for your essay must take place before you go in to take your test. You will likely have a basic idea of what the test will be about, so you must read the background material, your textbook, and any additional assigned readings as though you had to write a paper about the subject. You want to know what you are talking about so you can form opinions (your introduction and conclusion) and support them with clear evidence (the supporting paragraphs and examples that make up the body of your paper). These are the essential aims of studying anyway.

> Rose's upcoming test on the history of basketball will definitely include an essay question. The test is to be about the 1992–1993 basketball season, and it will focus primarily on the Eastern Conference teams. Rose studies her textbook and does extensive Internet research as well. She hopes for a question on Patrick Ewing and his greatness; she dreads a question on Dominique Wilkins. She struggles, she hopes, she dreams, but most of all, she prepares.

Step 2: Take the Test

Generally, an essay test will have more than two essay questions. If you look at the first essay question and don't know how to answer it, do not waste time attempting to finagle your way through. If you have extra time at the end of the test, you can go back, but it is best to focus your time on the questions you know how to answer.

Step 3: Outline Your Essay

These questions deserve very brief outlines. The outlines need not even be written down; nevertheless, they must be thought through. Do not make life needlessly difficult for yourself by writing without knowing what you are writing. Figure out your topic sentence, then your three examples; then you can begin.

Rose goes to class on the day of the test. She has extra pens in case one runs out of ink. She has gotten sufficient sleep the previous three nights. She is ready for anything. The test begins with true-or-false questions; she breezes through these. Then, the essay prompt reads: "Compare and contrast Patrick Ewing and Shaquille O'Neal as they performed over the course of the 1992–1993 basketball season, and decide which of the two you think should have been the starting center of the All-Star game."

She quickly writes:

> Ewing was the better center. (1) better leadership of team (2) more control over whole game, not just his performance, and (3) not a show-off.

Her outline is now complete; she is ready to start writing.

Step 4: Write the Essay

Essays written under timed conditions leave less room for posturing. The pressure of time forces you to think of what you want to say, say it, and proceed. This can lead to better writing in general, because you are forced to say what you mean. Do not be intimidated by those who sit at desks near yours and ask the teacher for additional blue books or paper. Length is not in and of itself a virtue. The more succinctly you express yourself, the better your essay will be, so do not spend time thinking about the fanciest way to write something, just write it.

In the paragraphs that make up the body of the essay (the exception being the one-paragraph essay in which you simply state the examples that support your conclusion), you must clearly present the supporting evidence, and then show how that evidence supports your point. It is not enough to say that there were high taxes on tea at the time and people in Boston were unhappy. You must also note that this demonstrates that there was ample reason for revolution.

INTRO

Two of the most important centers in the Eastern conference over the 1992–93 season were Patrick Ewing of the New York Knickerbockers and Shaquille O'Neal of the Orlando Magic. Both are magnificent athletes, and they have similarities as well as differences, but in any comparison, Patrick Ewing is a better center and deserved to start in the All-Star game.

COMPARE AND CONTRAST

The two players were very similar. Both were high-scoring centers, both excelled in the college game, and both were the number-one draft picks of their respective years. Yet it is important to note that these years were very different. O'Neal came out of the draft in 1992, so the 92–93 season was his first. Ewing was drafted in 1985. During the 1992–93 season Ewing was just reaching the height of his considerable powers. His experience and maturity would lend an important resonance to the Eastern All-Star team.

EWING BETTER

They both played the role of the outstanding player of their particular teams. But this role, and the ways they performed in it, also demonstrates some of their differences, and shows why, and how, Ewing was the more appropriate choice for All-Star center.

REASON 1

As the star of his team, Ewing did an outstanding job in scoring, rebounds, and assists. Thus, he not only played well for himself, making himself a better player, but he made his team a better team. One of the most important developments of the 92–93 season was the offensive presence of John Starks. Clearly, Starks could not have come to the fore unless Ewing had played in such a way as to help develop another outstanding player.

While some may say that Ewing was surrounded by better players, this is not enough to prove that the centers' differences resulted solely from their teams. Most glaring among O'Neal's weaknesses of that season was his self-congratulatory play. A smashed backboard may have looked impressive at the time, but it was only another piece of evidence showing that O'Neal wanted his playing to be noticed. Contrast that with Ewing, who never asked for attention, but worked his absolute hardest so that his team would be noticed, and win.

REASON 2

The many reasons mentioned here: experience in the National Basketball Association, leadership ability, and generous play, provide sufficient evidence that during the 1992–93 season, Patrick Ewing was a better center, and a better player, than Shaquille O'Neal, and thus would have been the best choice for the starting center for the Eastern All-Star team.

CONCLUSION

Step 5: Determine If Your Essay Answers the Question

This is *very important*. Sometimes you may go off on a tangent that interests you, and in doing so provide a strong base for your response to the question without actually answering it. If so, simply add a paragraph that more fully responds to what you have been asked.

Step 6: Proofread

While proofreading is always a part of writing, it takes a slightly different form in a test situation. You do not have much time, so you must restrict your check to flagrant errors of meaning and form. A sentence that expresses what you mean in a slightly awkward form does not have to be rewritten in a testing environment. If your teacher had intended you to create a perfectly written piece, he would have assigned theses topics as essays to take home rather than to be written under timed conditions in class. Your essay must (1) make sense, and (2) answer the question asked. These are your two main criteria when proofing.

Step 7: Hand That Baby In

And pat yourself on the back too—you did it.

Common Pitfalls

Before moving on, take a moment to review these common pitfalls for timed writing.

"Creative" Writing

There are some people who, even if caught red-handed with the Mona Lisa outside the Louvre Museum in Paris, would be able to talk our way out of the situation—in French. If this description does not fit you, do not attempt to talk your way out of not knowing the answer to an essay question.

Illegible Handwriting

Remember that the person who wrote this test needs to grade it as well, and if she cannot read what you wrote, then you likely will not get a high score, no matter how brilliant the content. Try to be aware of this as you write. Slow down, and if it will help, print instead of using cursive.

Too Many Examples

An essay usually calls for three examples. In some circumstances you may be called upon to present as many as five. Include more than five examples and your efforts will be counterproductive. The reader of your essay wants to know that you understand the subject and can back up your understanding with pertinent facts, observations, or illustrations. Going beyond this becomes tedious.

Formatting Your Essay

Essays on examinations require no particular format other than paragraph form. Be sure to indent and use full sentences.

When referring to a published work for the first time in an essay test, write the name of the book or article and the author. For subsequent references to that work, simply use the author's last name.

Recommended Reading

These books contain essays of a less personal nature than most. Any would be helpful to read for inspiration when writing a personal essay, or writing any sort of non-personal essay, such as a review, editorial, or creative nonfiction.

Mike Davis, *City of Quartz*, London Press.

M. F. K. Fisher, *The Art of Eating*, Collier Books.

Fran Lebowitz, *Social Studies*, Pocket Books, and Metropolitan Life, E.P. Dutton.

John McPhee, *The John McPhee Reader*, Farrar, Straus and Giroux.

Flannery O'Connor, *Mystery and Manners*, Noonday Press.

George Plimpton, *Hank Aaron: One For The Record*, Bantam Books.

William Strunk and E. B. White, *The Elements of Style*, Macmillan.

CHAPTER 7

Research Papers

Writing Research Papers

For many people, the research paper is the most daunting academic task. But rest assured, research papers are highly doable and can even be relatively painless when you have a clear plan of attack. If you follow the steps discussed in this chapter, writing a research paper is no more difficult than following an intricate recipe for chocolate cake.

Research Paper Format

A research paper is really just a long essay, so it will have the same basic construction.

Introduction

Some papers will ask you to prove some sort of argument and others will ask only for loads of information about a subject. If you are trying to prove a thesis, indicate that during the introduction. If you are writing a purely informative paper, set forth the subject of the paper in the introduction along with the aspects of the subject you intend to discuss.

Body

The body of the paper consists of the information you have garnered through your extensive research. In a paper that presents an argument, the body includes a cogent support of the argument. It also includes one section for the opposition's case, which you then endeavor to disprove. You make your own argument much more convincing by allowing the reader to see the counter-arguments made, and then a reasoned rebuttal of such.

In an informational paper, the body presents all the research on your subject, in a logical and organized manner.

Separate your research into themes, and then build the paper theme by theme, using paragraphs to separate them. In a paper that's more than 25 pages, paragraphing may not be sufficient to separate your themes. In that case, subsections may be necessary, and within those subsections you may need to create paragraphs. Whatever format you select, make sure you maintain it consistently throughout your paper.

Research papers also allow for other media such as photographs and illustrations, so the body of the paper often includes both text and visual material. Take full advantage of this and use them where appropriate to accent and allow the reader to attach visual images to the text. A research paper is like a long magazine article, and what usually interests you in long magazine articles? Not just the information presented, but also the manner in which it is displayed and—let's be honest here—the fancy pictures. A research paper should be interesting, and a pleasing layout can be an important part of that.

The body of the paper refers to sources quite regularly, as that is the aim of a research paper. Any direct quotes from sources or paraphrases from research sources are footnoted. This means, after a quote or paraphrase, put a number (these references will go in order of the paper), and at the bottom of the page, you write the source of the note, including title, author, publisher. You will find more information on how to write footnotes in the Specifics section of this chapter.

Conclusion

The conclusion restates the main point and indicates how the paper has accomplished it. If your paper argued for a particular thesis, reiterate how that thesis was proved by the successive examples. If your paper described a phenomenon, summarize the information presented and what it showed you.

Bibliography

One thing that distinguishes a research paper from other nonfiction writing is the inclusion of a bibliography. Here you will indicate the sources you used for the information you presented in the paper. Anything you read that aided you in your understanding of the subject is included here, according to the guidelines described later in this chapter.

Writing the Paper

Step 1: Select Your Topic or Thesis

Some teachers may assign a specific topic, but most will provide a possible range and allow you to select your own. A research paper is an opportunity for your teacher or professor to assess your research and writing skills. Typically, your instructor will assign a paper of some specified length—5, 10, or 20 pages—on a variety of topics. "Cover some important issue about Colonial history in the early 1800s," she might say. It is then up to you to select the exact topic, find out all there is to know about it, and write the thing. For instance, our friend Tim might be assigned a paper.

> Tim is taking a class in nutritional sociology and his teacher announces, "A five-page research paper on some way sugar's influence is seen in our society, due in one month. I expect you to research and annotate this responsibly."

The most important criteria for a topic are its interest to you and the breadth of the topic.

Interest to You

If the topic you select holds no appeal, it is very doubtful your paper will be interesting to you or your reader. This can lead to problems, because if you are not interested, it will be that much more difficult to get yourself to write the darn thing, and what you do write will not be your best. Even if the range of topics does not light your fire, try to find an angle that does. You may not be interested in the Reconstruction-era South, but you may be interested in the race relations, health care, or leisure activities of that time. A bit of research here into the range of topics from which you have to choose can be extremely beneficial. Read for things that catch your interest. Look at titles of books for ideas on what other writers have been interested in; you may be inspired.

> Tim reads up on sugar at the library. He talks to people in the street about sugar. He eats a packet of sugar straight out of the sugar bowl in a restaurant, provoking complaints to the management from other customers. He listens to "A spoonful of sugar makes the medicine go down" and briefly considers writing his paper about sugar in the modern American musical; his research is blocked by his inability to find any other references to sugar in musicals, with the notable exception of *Charlie and the Chocolate Factory*, which he finds frighteningly hallucinatory. He is seen walking through the street clutching a bag of sugar and shaking his head, bewildered.

Breadth of Topic

This is generally the stickiest issue when writing a paper. You want your topic to be small enough to cover in a paper, but broad enough that you can wring 10 or 20 pages out of it. Though you would be astounded on what people can base a 200-page book, a paper on the Reconstruction-era south would probably need closer to 1,000 pages, while the sash of Robert E. Lee's uniform would probably fill only one good paragraph.

> Tim briefly considers a paper about sugar in general, then goes to the library and finds 250 books on that topic. Too many. He regroups and considers a paper about the first bite of a candy bar; is it different from the other bites? He returns to the library, finds nothing.

Step 2: Get Your Topic Approved

Before you begin searching for the perfect quote, make sure the topic you have chosen is an acceptable one. Few things are worse than starting a huge bulk of research or writing only to find out that it was all for nothing. If your topic is off the mark, your teacher or professor can guide you to one more suitable. You can't lose by asking.

Frustrated, Tim visits his teacher after class. "The first bite of a candy bar?" she asks.

"Yes," says Tim. "It's the part of a candy bar I like the best."

"Well," the teacher says, "if it's candy bars you're interested in, why don't you write your paper on that? I myself am a Milky Way fan. I love nougat."

Tim ponders this. Could it be, he wonders, that specific personality types like specific types of candy bars? He proposes this thesis to his teacher. Intrigued, she approves his paper topic.

Step 3: Conduct the Research

Your main task is to find out as much as you can about your topic. You may be writing a research paper in which you are arguing for one thesis or another, or you may be describing a particular situation or phenomenon. Find as much material as possible about your topic. Your librarian can help you, if needed. Librarians are great resources and are usually very willing to offer assistance.

It is not necessary for you to read every word of every book or article you find. Once you have amassed a collection, look through the tables of contents of the books and read those chapters that seem applicable. Look in the bibliography of these books for suggestions of other books that might be helpful.

As you collect your reference material, you should start taking notes. It is imperative that your notes be taken in an organized manner, because often this stage of the paper allows you to get your thinking done, and the more organized and clear your thinking, the better your paper. For each book or article you read, you should have a separate set of cards. At the top of each card put the title of the book from which the notes were gathered.

Then, at the top right corner of the card, mark how this note applies to your paper. This can be even easier if you use color coding. For instance, if your paper describes the secret lives of presidents, you might put the title of the book on the left, *The Best and the Brightest,* and on the right a red mark, indicating that this book is about Kennedy. Keep a master list explaining all your color codes and other reference marks in case you confuse yourself. Writing down quotes from books that strike you as important or particularly relevant is also helpful. Noting the page number here will come in handy when you want to footnote. Set aside a list of illustrations and photographs related to your subject.

Tim spends the next two weeks at the library, poring over psychiatric journals and candy wrappers. He sets up a complex cross-coding system involving colors and shapes. Cards related to daring types he marks with a triangle, stay-at-homes he marks with a square, tormented souls get a circle. Caramel candy bars are yellow, mint is green, mixtures are purple.

Nougat Quarterly ○

According to Professor Whipt, those who like nougat are often confused as to what nougat actually consists of, and what the difference is between caramel and nougat. Many teens admitted to eating nougat before listening to heavy metal music and getting body piercings. Connection??? "Nougat seemed to be the only substance to offer the subjects comfort." p. 73, article titled "An important study."

Tim has been working feverishly at the library. So thrilled is he by Professor Whipt's article that he found three more articles by Whipt written in the past year. Tim collects fifty cards; his confidence grows. He knows he has something here.

Step 4: Make an Outline

Once you have most of your research completed, you are ready to begin your outline.

An outline is absolutely indispensable for a research paper because it gives you an idea of what you are writing and what you need to write next. It also breaks your paper up into distinct parts, which will guide your writing process as well as allow you to write sections out of order. Bored with writing one section? Check your outline and start working on a different section that seems more interesting.

An outline is a sort of annotated table of contents for your research paper, and writing this outline provides you with an opportunity to organize your thoughts and your paper. The outline then provides you with a structure.

Write Your Statement of Purpose

You already have an idea of the subject of your paper, now you need to describe this subject with some sort of concise statement. For example: The purpose of this paper is to compare the courting rituals of men and women in 21st-century urban areas.

Organize Your Cards

Separate your cards into the order in which you want to refer to their topics. Depending on the length of your paper, you may have 3 to 30 subcategories. Try to organize them so that related subjects are close together, and there is some sort of natural transition between paragraphs.

Write Your Conclusion

We know, you've already written your statement of purpose in the first part of the outline, but it can only help to make it clearer to yourself, and the conclusion should refer to the organizational structure you've set up to support it.

While at home with his note cards, Tim contemplates his research. Just what is his thesis? What does his research lead him to? He knows there is a psychology to which chocolate bars different people choose, but what is it? He writes:

Thesis: Candy bars and personality—is there a connection? Yes.

Tim consults his note cards and orders them into a logical thought process.

I. Psychology has long posited that there is a strong connection between the types of foods we eat and our psyches.
   A. Hogg's study of food and society
      1. Quote about judging society by food on card 2
      2. How long study went on
   B. Weird nutritional shakes in American society
      1. Calvinist
   C. Food preferences of people throughout history
      1. Pres. Clinton
      2. Romans
II. Nutty Nougat, other mixed versions
   A. People desperate for action
III. Caramels
   A. Sentimentality
      1. Quote on card 7
IV. Nut bars
   A. The tough guy: peanuts and machismo
V. Solid chocolate bar
   A. High-minded? or
   B. Repressed?
VI. Coconut bars
   A. Sometimes you feel like a nut?
      1. Psychopaths and coconut
VII. Butter Krisp, toffee bars, Tasty Toffee
   A. Are they really classier than the rest of us?

VIII. The opposition, the idea of taste as personal issue
   A.   Card 24, Dr. Faust says there is no connection, we all have free will
   B.   Card 26, Dr. Schmidt says taste changes over eras
IX. Rebuttal
   A.   Swiss studies, television commercials
   B.   Fashion analogy
X.   Conclusion: The connection between candy bars and personality cannot be ignored, and allows us all to know more about sugar and the world we live in, and the way it affects us.

Tim sets his paper down next to the ordered cards, places his books next to them, and takes a well-deserved break.

Step 5: Check Your Plan

When your outline is finished, you should have a paragraph-by-paragraph plan of action. Do you know what each paragraph is to be about? Does each paragraph support your statement of purpose? If the topic of the paper is in the form of a question, does your outline answer it? When you can answer yes to these questions, you are officially ready to write.

Step 6: Write a Rough Draft

Many writers prefer to leave the writing of their introductory paragraph till the end, when they know exactly what they will be introducing. You probably want to start writing the paragraph that will follow the introduction, the paragraph in which you begin discussion of the topic. Here, your research index cards will come in handy. You already have your cards organized for each paragraph; now use them, making clear your quotes and paraphrases with footnotes, and presenting the findings of all that research. Follow your outline carefully, going paragraph by paragraph, keeping your cards in order for easy reference by the end. Give yourself plenty of time; burnout and exhaustion lead to sloppy writing. When you get to the end you can write your introductory and conclusive paragraphs, which will be fairly similar.

Step 7: Take a Break (or a Day Off), Then Reread and Edit the Paper

Once you have written your paper according to the form of your outline, you have what is known as the first draft. You will probably want to take a day off after finishing the first draft to give yourself some breathing room before you come back to edit it. Make sure one paragraph flows smoothly to the next. Make sure you have given credit where credit is due. When paraphrasing or quoting you MUST credit the source, inserting footnotes as you go along.

Questions to Ask When You Are Editing Your Paper

- Do I make a convincing case for my point?
- Do I present the story of whatever I'm describing in an interesting and engaging manner?
- Are both my arguments and the opposition's arguments clearly presented?
- Does each paragraph serve a clear function either in describing the phenomenon or arguing the case?
- Do the sentences flow logically?
- Does each sentence serve a clear function in its paragraph?

If you find an unnecessary paragraph or sentence, eliminate it. If you have not made your point, look to find where you have strayed from your outline. Rewrite any illogical sentences. If you have a trusted friend, you may want to have her read it. This is all a lot of work, but it is work that is absolutely essential for a good paper. Also check for misspellings and grammatical mistakes. Make sure you read your paper through at least twice, correcting errors as you go along. Once you have edited and cleaned up any errors, you are ready for the final touches.

Editing Drill

Edit Tim's five-page paper, referring back to the editing guidelines in Chapter 4. Then compare your edits with ours in the section following this paper.

Candy Bars and Psychology

Psychology has long posited a connection between the psyche and taste in food. The noted professor of food and psychology, Liz Onya, says, "While many attempt to discover the secrets of the mind through outmoded techniques of psychoanalysis and clinical psychology, the true frontier on which we are discovering the key to personality is by assessing what people eat. Beyond this we cannot hope to go further." (WRITE IN FOOTNOTE FOR ONYA's STUDY) Onya's studies relating diet and psychosis went on for over twenty-five years, and they clearly show what any reasonable person has long suspected: you are what you eat. Think of the current fad of liquid diet shakes, so appropriate to our American society, caught between the Calvinist puritanism of our history and the relentless greed and self-indulgence of our current market economy. Consider former President Clinton and his fondness for fast food, the food of a person of action, someone ready to lead! Or remember the self-destructive habits of the romans, fulfilling the slightest desire with loads of tempting delicacies, then running off to the vomitoria to rid themselves and begin again. This demonstrates a clear connection between what one eats and who one is. And indeed, the existence of a connection between food and personality points to the likelihood of a connection between candy bar choice and personality disorder.

Many studies have been done to test this theory and the results of them are here.

Much has been written about those candy bars that combine the various candy elements: nougat, caramel, nuts. The desire for all the things at once, the inability to make any sort of a concrete choice is typical of the boy/ man who suffers from the peter pan syndrome, and the combination bar is his candy of choice. This is evidenced on grounds both academic and emotional. In her ground-breaking treatise on the subject, Dr. Lotta Kaloreese inter-viewed a group of 2,500 male participants between the ages of 23 and 55. Of those who said they were either involved or willing to be involved in what they themselves termed a mature lifestyle, only 19.7% indicated the com-bination bar, or "Nutty Nougat," as their primary candy choice. Of those who professed a longing to return to childhood, or to remain a child indefinitely, an astonishing 78% indicated a strong preference for the Nutty Nougat bar as their primary candy choice. (CITE KALOREESE'S STUDY) Numerical results this overwhelming cannot be ignored: Nutty Nougat is the bar of those who would be children forever.

Another stunning example is the historical references of the caramel. One of the most traditional forms of con-fection, the caramel is the choice of those who are overly sentimental and prone to emotional outbursts and flights of fancy. Many soft-hearted artists have long called the caramel their favorite, with laudatory remarks often taking the form of song and poetry. "Boy, there's nothing a like better than a chocolate bar with caramel in it." (CHECK MLA, DO I NEED TO FOOTNOTE THIS IF I HAVE HIS NAME?) says Ima Mush, renowned emotional person. This sort of confession is seen over and over again in memoirs of emotional people. This happens too frequently to be mere happenstance, one has yet another reason to believe that there must be some connection between the form of candy sugar takes, and the type of person who wants that candy.

Yet another example is apparent in the strong connection between nut bars and those who love them, the tough guys both male and female. While much has been written on the connection between nuts of all types and risk-taking daredevils, including the tie between skydiving and various types of nut brittle, the clearest delineation of candy to personality is peanuts to machismo. The study was done is most particularly seen in the desire of river guides, hunters, and rock climbers for Mr. Chocobar, the peanut chocolate bar. (RICH) Dr. Rich performed his study over two years in all the venues mentioned. He used three groups among each participants. To the first group he offered a buffet table at the end of their trips which contained fruit, chocolate bars of assorted types other than Mr. Chocobars, arranged with the Mr. Chocobars at the back less reachable part of the table, with the fruit and other candy toward the front. The participants—94% of them—reached to the back to get their Mr. Chocobars. Several, 62% of those who chose the Mr. Chocobar, were heard to grunt the word "Choco." Upon taking the bar. Dr. Rich considered the possibility that these participants had chosen the bars because they were at the back and therefore more difficult to reach and therefore a greater "prize" to these rough and tumble participants, and to try to weed these out he set up another buffet at which the Mr. Chocobars were set near the front in easy reach, no challenge at all. Again an overwhelming majority, 86% this time, chose the Mr. Chocobar over any other candy. His final group was served with a mixed buffet on which the candy was arranged every which way, with the results the same. This buffet was, in fact, picked clean of all peanut related candy, with fruit and other candy left strewn apart, due, he hypothesizes, to the desire of "macho" individuals for a hunt for their prey. On returning to his University to organize and publish his findings he tried a control group, and offered an audience of 2,000 anthropology students the same buffet. Only an astonishing 21% chose the Mr. Chocobar, and the candy proportions were the same. There can be no clearer evidence than this that there is indeed, a correlation between candy type and personality.

Scientific reason would lead one to consider whether this applied to only the nut bar, or the caramel. Recent research in the chocolate bar field has uncovered some startling findings. People who purchase the plain chocolate and milk chocolate bars generally complain of a feeling of a life left unfulfilled, of feelings and possibilities left unexplored. (WHOEVER) Similar studies of randomly selected buyers of toffee bars, including the Tasty Toffee and the Score bar indicate that these buyers, or at least 89% of these buyers, can be classified as suffering from superiority complexes, defined as the strong belief that they are better than the rest of us. The compelling evidence linking the lover of coconut bars and the psychopath only cements the bond.

There are many in both the scientific and confectionery community who protest that chocolate bar preference is merely a matter of personal taste, and hence unrelated to any personality quirks. Most notable among these groups are Dr. Faust and Dr. Schmidt. Dr. Faust notes that much as the experiments have done to set up control groups, the studies done have not covered a wide enough expanse of the population. (FOOTNOTE? OR LATER ON?) In fact, all the studies, he notes, have been done in the United States where the candy bars advertise their images via television commercials. Thus it is these media images of the bars that people respond to, not the bars themselves. Dr. Schmidt notes in his book, Candy Bars and Personality: There's No Connection, that candy bars and what goes in them changes over time, for instance licorice is not nearly as popular as it was in the early forties. (SCHMIDT) This change over time indicates to her that there is no real correlation, because that would indicate a change in human personality type within the space of a decade, and this she considers unlikely.

While these doctors are to be commended for their dogged attempts to discover the truth, their arguments cannot withstand scientific scrutiny. Dr. Faust is correct in noting that the studies have been done for the most part in the United States, but he ignores the important Swiss chocolate series of the Kiss Institute and the Mousse inquiries of the Academie francaise de bonbons. As for his contention that television affects the subjects ability to respond in an unbiased manner toward the candy bar, he forgets that the images subjects respond to are not those projected by the candy company. For instance, as discussed earlier, Mr. Chocobar is loved by those who attempt to prove their prowess in sports and outdoor pursuits, yet the advertised image of Mr. Chocobar is as a friendly "fun" sort of candy bar, associated with young children and spotted dogs. Clearly, the subjects are not getting their ides from television, as Dr. Faust suggests. As for Dr. Schmidt's allegations, just because tastes and associations change over time does not mean that there is no connection but rather that there is a connection and that it is mutable. One would not argue that fashion decisions have no ties to personality, clearly what one wears says a lot about who one is, yet these choices also change over time.

The experiments of Dr. Kaloreese and Dr. Rich show Dr. Onya's belief regarding the relationship between candy bar choice and personality to be true. In fact, their findings serve as scientific proof for the connection. This evidence, along with one's own sense of taste as a function of persona belie the claims of skeptics and demonstrate that Onya's words are true.

"Though many will fight me on this, and scores of others will cover their eyes and ears to ignore the knowledge I bring, I will stay on this earth loudly proclaiming what I know to be the truth: as a man lives, so does he eat, and as he chooses candy, so do we know his most private self."

Our Version, With Edits

Here is the version marked with the edits we thought were necessary. Are they the same as your edits? Don't worry if they aren't, but check for differences to see the reasoning behind them.

Candy Bars and Psychology

Psychology has long posited a connection between the

ww
"preference"

psyche and (taste) in food. The noted professor of food

move to
beginning of
sentence

and psychology, Dr. (Liz Onya) says, "While many attempt to discover the secrets of the mind through outmoded techniques of psychoanalysis and clinical psychology, the true frontier on which we are discovering the key to personality

ment of

is by assessing what people eat. Beyond this, we cannot hope to go further." (WRITE IN FOOTNOTE FOR ONYA's STUDY) Onya's studies relating diet and psychosis went on

every *do not*
use "you"

for over twenty-five years, and they clearly show what any reasonable person has long suspected: (you are what you) eat. Think of the current fad of liquid diet shakes, so appro-

as it is

priate to our American society, caught between the Calvin-

agreement

its

ist puritanism of our history and the relentless greed and

this is in
addition
to—use
"and" or
remove
entirely

self-indulgence of our current market economy. Consider former President Clinton and his fondness for fast food, the food of a person of action, someone ready to lead. (Or) remember the self-destructive habits of the romans, fulfilling the slightest desire with loads of tempting delica-

All these

cies, then running off to the vomitoria to rid themselves and begin again. (This) demonstrates a clear connection between what one eats and who one is. And indeed, the

maybe begin the sentence
with this

existence of a connection between food and personality
points to the likelihood of a connection between candy bar

awk, need better
transition sentence

choice and ~~personality disorder.~~

~~Many studies have been done to test this theory and the results of them are here.~~

extra

Much has been written about ~~those~~ candy bars that
combine the various candy elements: nougat, caramel,
nuts. The desire for all the things at once, the inability to
make any sort of a concrete choice is typical of the boy/
man who suffers from the peter pan syndrome, and the
combination bar is his candy of choice. ~~This is evidenced~~

put this
later

There is both

evidence

~~on grounds both~~ academic and emotional. In her ground-
breaking treatise on ~~the~~ this subject, Dr. Lotta Kaloreese inter-
viewed ~~a group of~~ 2,500 male participants between the

unnecessary

ages of 23 and 55. Of those who said they ~~were either
involved or willing to be involved in what they themselves~~
termed a "mature lifestyle," only 19.7% indicated the combination bar, or "Nutty Nougat," as their primary candy
choice. Of those who professed a longing to return to
childhood, or to remain a child indefinitely, an astonishing
78% indicated a strong preference for the Nutty Nougat
bar as their primary candy choice. (CITE KALOREESE'S
STUDY) Numerical results this overwhelming cannot be
ignored: Nutty Nougat is the ~~bar of those who would be
children forever.~~ the eternal child

repetitive

Another stunning example is the historical references
of the caramel. One of the most traditional forms of con-
fection, the caramel is the choice of those who are overly

ould
egin with
his and
ork up to
ombination

sentimental and prone to emotional outbursts and flights of fancy. Many soft-hearted artists have long called the caramel their favorite, with laudatory remarks often taking the form of song and poetry. "Boy, there's nothing ~~I~~ like better than a chocolate bar with caramel in it." (CHECK MLA, DO I NEED TO FOOTNOTE THIS IF I HAVE HIS NAME?) says Ima Mush, renowned emotional person. This sort of confession is seen over and over again in memoirs of ~~emotional~~ the sentimental ~~(people.)~~ This happens too frequently to be mere happenstance, *and* one has yet another reason to believe that there must be some connection between the form of candy sugar takes, and the type of person who wants that candy.

repetition (people, person)

Yet another example is apparent in the strong connection between nut bars and those who love them,"the tough guys"both male and female. While much has been written on the connection between nuts of all types and risk-taking daredevils, including the tie between skydiving and various types of nut brittle, the clearest (delineation) of candy ~~to~~ *and* personality is peanuts to machismo. ~~The study~~ ~~was done is most particularly seen in the~~ desire of river guides, hunters, and rock climbers for Mr. Chocobar, the (peanut chocolate bar.)(RICH) Dr. Rich ~~performed his study~~ *studied them for* over two years ~~in~~(all the venues)~~mentioned~~ He ~~used three~~ ~~groups among each~~ participants, *divided the into three groups* ~~To the first group~~

the connection between

why the fancy word? use instance

suggest replacing with "A study was done to examine the..."

reword

too much

precede this sentence with the other sentence ending in "river guides, hunters, etc."

[handwritten: arranged to have] *[handwritten: for the first group,]*

he ~~offered~~ a buffet table ~~at the end of their trips~~ (which) *[handwritten: unnecessary]* contained *[ing]* fruit, chocolate bars of assorted types other than Mr. Chocobars, ~~arranged with the~~ Mr. Chocobars ate ~~the back~~ less reachable, part of the table, with the fruit and other candy toward the front. The participants—94% of them—reached to the back to get ~~their~~ Mr. Chocobars. *[handwritten margin: arranged so the Mr. Chocobars were in a remote,]* *[handwritten: already understood]*

~~Several,~~ 62% of those ~~who chose the Mr. Chocobar~~ were heard to grunt the word "Choco." Upon taking the ~~bar~~ candy, Dr. Rich considered the possibility that these participants had chosen the bars because they were at the back and therefore more difficult to reach and therefore a greater "prize" to these rough and tumble participants, ~~and~~ to try to weed these out he set up another buffet at which the Mr. Chocobars were set near the front in easy reach, no challenge at all. Again an overwhelming majority, 86% this time, chose ~~the~~ Mr. Chocobar over any other candy. His final group was served with a mixed buffet on which the candy was arranged every which way, ~~with~~ the results were the same. This buffet was, in fact, picked clean of all peanut related candy, with fruit and other candy left strewn ~~apart~~ about due, he hypothesized, to the desire of "macho" individuals for a hunt for their prey. On returning to his University to organize and publish his findings Dr. Rich tried a control group, and offered an audience of 2,000 anthropology students the same buffet. Only an astonishing 21% chose the Mr. Chocobar, and from a selection in which the candy proportions were the same. There can be no clearer evidence than this that there is, indeed, a correlation between candy type and personality.

[handwritten margin: not only did this overwhelming majority choose Mr. Chocobars but,] *[handwritten: candy,]* *[handwritten: He used his second group]* *[handwritten: were]* *[handwritten: about]* *[handwritten: should footnote this]* *[handwritten: Dr. Rich]* *[handwritten: to A section on the next page]*

Scientific reason would lead one to consider whether this applied to only the nut bar, or the caramel. Recent research in the chocolate bar field has uncovered some startling findings. People who purchase ~~the~~ plain chocolate and milk chocolate bars generally complain of a feeling of a life left unfulfilled, of feelings and possibilities left unexplored. (WHOEVER) Similar studies of randomly selected buyers of toffee bars, including the Tasty Toffee and the Score bar indicate that these buyers, or at least 89% of these buyers, can be classified as suffering from superiority complexes, defined as the strong belief that they are better than the rest of (us.) The compelling evidence linking the lover of coconut bars and the psychopath only cements the bond.

do not personalize

Ⓐ

Nevertheless, There are many in both the scientific and confectionery community who protest that chocolate bar preference is *pompous? change* merely a matter of personal taste, and (hence) unrelated to any personality quirks. ~~Most~~ notable among these ~~groups~~ *is* ~~are~~ Dr. Faust ~~and Dr. Schmidt~~. Dr. Faust notes that much as the experiments have done to set up control groups, the studies done have not covered a wide enough expanse of the population. (FOOTNOTE? OR LATER ON?) In fact, all the studies, he notes, have been done in the United States where the candy bars *companies* advertise their images via television commercials. *he maintains,* Thus it is these media images of the bars that people respond to, not the bars themselves. Dr. *another opponent of candy and personality theory,* Schmidt notes in his book, [Candy Bars and Personality: There's No Connection,] that candy bars and what goes in *to*

doubt the detractors

introduce him later with his theory

them change over time, for instance, licorice is not nearly as popular as it was in the early forties. (SCHMIDT) This change over time indicates to her that there is no real correlation, that would indicate a change in human personality type within the space of a decade, and this she considers unlikely.

too much? While these doctors are to be commended for their ⟨dogged⟩ attempts to discover the truth, their arguments cannot withstand scientific scrutiny. Dr. Faust is correct in noting that the studies have been done for the most part in the United States, but he ignores the important Swiss chocolate series of the Kiss Institute, *as well as* the Mousse inquiries of the Academie francaise, de bonbons. As for his contention that television affects the subjects ability to respond in an unbiased manner toward the candy bar, he forgets that the images subjects respond to are *need to have a sentence of explanation for what these studies are and what they show* not those projected by the candy company. For instance, as discussed earlier, Mr. Chocobar is loved by those who attempt to prove their prowess in sports and outdoor pursuits, yet the advertised image of Mr. Chocobar is as a friendly "fun" sort of candy bar, associated with young children and spotted dogs. Clearly, the subjects are not getting their idea from television, as Dr. Faust suggests. As for Dr. Schmidt's allegations, just because tastes and associations change over time does not mean that there is no connection, rather, that there is a connection and *it implies* *ital?*

~~that~~It is mutable. One would not argue that fashion deci-

sions have no ties to personality, clearly what one wears

says ~~a lot~~ *a great deal* about who one is, yet these choices also change

over time.

decide
personality or
personality
disorder
The experiments of Dr. Kaloreese and Dr. Rich show

Dr. Onya's belief regarding the relationship between candy

bar choice and (personality) to be true. In fact, their find-

ings serve as scientific proof for the connection. This evi-

dence, along with one's own sense of taste as a function of

persona, belie the claims of skeptics and demonstrate that

Onya's words are true.

"Though many will fight me on this, and scores of oth-

ers will cover their eyes and ears to ignore the knowledge

I bring, I will stay on this earth loudly proclaiming what I

know to be the truth: as a man lives, so does he eat, and

as he chooses candy, so do we know his most private self."

Once you have made all the edits, both organizational and stylistic, you are ready to put your paper into its final stages, complete with reference and format specifications. This work is mostly mechanical, but it does require that you pay close attention to minute details. The end is in sight, but don't let that allow you a sloppy finish.

Step 8: Create a Bibliography

A bibliography is the list of references used in the writing of a paper. Compile your bibliography according to the rules of whatever style guide you are using, whether MLA, APA, or Chicago. Citation style is usually determined by your instructor, so be sure to ask if you're not sure! Note that in the final draft of Tim's research paper beginning on the next page, Chicago style is used.

Step 9: Title Your Paper

Finally, when the rest of the paper is sitting on your desk all clean and edited with bibliography, you can create a title. For some reason, academic papers tend to have titles with colons in them.

Spiderman: Arachnid or Anarchist?

Stalin, Hitler, and Mussolini:
People I'm Glad I Didn't Know

And so forth. Your title should indicate the subject of your paper in a pithy manner, and, if possible, be eye-catching. Don't be afraid to have some fun with this; it's the part of your paper your teacher sees first and should be as interesting as you can make it.

Step 10: Write Your Final Draft

Sometimes You Feel Like A Nut, Sometimes You Don't:
Candy Bars and the Psychology of Taste
by Tim

Psychology has long posited a connection between the psyche and food preferences. Noted professor of food and psychology Liz Onya says, "While many attempt to discover the secrets of the mind through outmoded techniques of psychoanalysis and clinical psychology, the true frontier on which we are discovering the key to personality is an assessment of what people eat."[1] Onya's studies relating diet and psychosis went on for over twenty-five years, and they clearly show what every reasonable person has long suspected: one is what one eats. Think of the current fad of liquid diet shakes, so appropriate to American society, caught as it is between the Calvinist puritanism of its history and the relentless greed and self-indulgence of its current market economy. Consider former President Clinton and his fondness for fast food, the food of a person of action, someone ready to lead! Remember the self-destructive habits of the Romans, fulfilling the slightest desire with loads of tempting delicacies, then running off to the vomitoria to rid themselves and begin again. All these demonstrate a clear connection between what one eats and who one is. Further, the existence of a

---

[1] Liz Onya, *Let's Eat Some More* (New York: Glutton & Sons, 1994), 107.

connection between food and personality points to the likelihood of a connection between candy bar choice and personality disorder.

This theory has been tested time and time again, and the results of these tests coincide: there is a connection. One of the earliest such studies explored the historical references of the caramel. Perhaps the most traditional form of confection, the caramel is the choice of those who are overly sentimental and prone to emotional outbursts and flights of fancy. Many soft-hearted artists have long called the caramel their favorite, with laudatory remarks often taking the form of song and poetry. "Boy, there's nothing I like better than a chocolate bar with caramel in it."[2] says Ima Mush, renowned emotional person. This sort of confession is seen over and over again in memoirs of emotional people. This happens too frequently to be mere happenstance, yet another reason to believe that there must be some connection between the form of candy sugar takes, and the type of person who wants that candy.

Much has also been written about candy bars that combine the various candy elements: nougat, caramel, nuts. The desire for all things at once, the inability to make

---

[2] Ima Mush, *Notes on a Sentimental Life* (Hawaii: Soft Hearts & Company, 1993), 21.

any sort of a concrete choice is typical of the boy/man who suffers from the Peter Pan syndrome, and the combination bar is his candy of choice. There is both academic and emotional evidence. In her ground-breaking treatise on this subject, Dr. Lotta Kaloreese interviewed 2,500 male participants between the ages of 23 and 55. Of those who said they lived what they termed a "mature lifestyle," only 19.7% indicated the combination bar, or "Nutty Nougat," as their primary candy choice. Of those who professed a longing to return to childhood or to remain a child indefinitely, an astonishing 78% indicated a strong preference for the Nutty Nougat bar as their primary candy choice.[3] Numerical results this overwhelming cannot be ignored: Nutty Nougat is the bar of the eternal child.

Yet another example is apparent in the strong connection between nut bars and those who love them, the "tough guys," both male and female. While much has been written on the connection between nuts of all types and risk-taking daredevils, including the tie between sky-diving and various types of nut brittle, the clearest instance of candy's connection to personality is the tie between peanuts and machismo. A study was commissioned to examine the common desire among river guides, hunters,

---

[3] Lotta Kaloreese, "Men Who Would Be Children" in *Experiments in Chocolate,* ed. Russell Upsom Grubb (Pennsylvania: Bar Press, 1991), 32–45.

Writing Smart

and rock climbers for the Mr. Chocobar, a chocolate bar with peanuts.[4] Dr. Rich divided the participants into three groups and studied them over two years. He arranged to have a buffet table for the first group, containing fruit and chocolate bars of assorted types, including Mr. Chocobars. He designed the buffet so the Mr. Chocobars were in a remote, less reachable part of the table. The participants—94% of them—reached to the back to get a Mr. Chocobar. Not only did this overwhelming majority select Mr. Chocobar, but 62% of those who chose the Mr. Chocobar were heard to grunt the word "Choco" upon taking the candy. Dr. Rich considered the possibility that these participants had chosen the bars because they were at the back and more difficult to reach, therefore a greater "prize" to these rough-and-tumble participants. He used his second group to try to weed these out. He set up another buffet at which the Mr. Chocobars were set near the front in easy reach, no challenge at all. Again an overwhelming majority, 86% this time, chose Mr. Chocobar over any other candy. His final group was served with a mixed buffet on which the candy was arranged every which way, and the results were the same. This buffet was, in fact, picked clean of all peanut-related candy, with fruit and other candy left strewn about, due, he hypothesized, to the desire of "macho"

---

[4]   Tu Rich, *Peanuts and Machismo* (Texas: Men Don't Press, 1993), 10.

individuals for a hunt for their prey. On returning to his university to organize and publish his findings, Dr. Rich examined a control group. He offered an audience of 2,000 anthropology students the same buffet. Only 21% chose the Mr. Chocobar from a selection in which the candy proportions were the same.

Scientific curiosity would lead one to consider whether this connection between personality and preference applied only to the nut bar and the caramel. Recent research in the chocolate bar field has uncovered some startling findings. People who purchase plain chocolate and milk chocolate bars generally complain of a feeling of a life left unfulfilled, of feelings and possibilities left unexplored.[5] Similar studies of randomly selected buyers of toffee bars, including the Tasty Toffee and the Score bar, indicate that at least 89% of these buyers suffer from superiority complexes, defined as the strong belief that they are better than the rest of the population. The compelling evidence linking the lover of coconut bars and the psychopath only cements the bond. There can be no clearer evidence than this that there is, indeed, a correlation between candy type and personality.

Nevertheless, there are many in both the scientific and confectionery communities who protest that chocolate bar preference is merely a matter of personal taste,

---

[5] Hy Phat, "The Life I Could Have Had: Plain Chocolate and the Repressed" in *Watchamacallit and Aphasia: A Journal of Chocolate and Mental Health,* ed. Roland Butter (Arizona: Bench Press, 1992).

Writing Smart

and therefore unrelated to any personality quirks. Notable among these is Dr. Faust. Dr. Faust notes that, much as the experimenters have tried to set up control groups, none of the studies have covered a wide enough expanse of the population.[6] Furthermore, Dr. Faust adds, the studies have all been conducted in the United States, where the candy bar companies advertise their images via television commercials. Thus, he maintains, people in the United States respond to these media images, not to the bars themselves. Dr. Schmidt, another opponent of candy-personality theory, notes in her book *Candy Bars and Personality: There's No Connection* that candy bars, and what goes into them, change over time. For instance, licorice is not nearly as popular as it was in the early forties.[7] This change over time indicates to her that there is no real correlation, because that would indicate a change in human personality type within the space of a century, and this she considers unlikely.

While Faust and Schmidt are to be commended for their dogged attempts to discover the truth, their arguments cannot withstand scientific scrutiny. Dr. Faust is correct in noting that the studies have been conducted for the most part in the United States, but he ignores the

---

[6] Goethe Faust, "I'd Sell My Soul to Publish a Book About Candy" in *Dubious Arguments* (Chicago: Arguers Anonymous Press, 1998), 14–23.
[7] I. Schmidt, *Candy Bars and Personality: There's No Connection* (New York: Skeptics & Company, 1988), 34–35.

important Swiss chocolate series of the Kiss Institute, as well as the Mousse inquiries of the Académie francaise de bonbons.[8] The Kiss Institute found the same superiority connection referred to earlier, displayed by over 500 participants from France, Switzerland, and Germany. The Mousse inquiries provided convincing evidence for the claim that various forms of mousse can be used in the treatment of many types of neuroses, establishing another clear connection between the psyche and chocolate. As for Dr. Faust's contention that television affects the subject's ability to respond in an unbiased manner toward the candy bar, he does not consider that the images projected by the candy company are unrelated to the interests and aspirations of the candy devotees. For instance, as discussed earlier, Mr. Chocobar is loved by those who attempt to prove their prowess in sports and outdoor pursuits, yet the advertised image of Mr. Chocobar is as a friendly "fun" sort of candy bar, associated with young children and spotted dogs. Clearly, the subjects are not getting their ideas from television, though Dr. Faust believes otherwise. As for Dr. Pheelgud's allegations, just because tastes and associations change over time does not mean that there is no connection between the two. It implies, rather, that there *is* a connection and it is mutable. One would not argue that fashion decisions have no ties to personality, clearly

---

8   Miss Swiss, *The Mousse Inquiries* (Switzerland: Braids & Company, 1962).

what one wears says a great deal about who one is, yet these choices also change over time.

The experiments of Dr. Kaloreese and Dr. Rich show Dr. Onya's belief regarding the relationship between candy bar choice and personality to be true. In fact, their findings serve as scientific proof for the connection. This evidence, along with one's own sense of taste as a function of persona, belie the claims of skeptics and demonstrate the truth of Onya's words. "Though many will fight me on this, and scores of others will cover their eyes and ears to ignore the knowledge I bring, I will stay on this earth loudly proclaiming what I know to be the truth: as a man lives, so does he eat, and as he chooses candy, so do we know his most private self."[9]

---

[9] Onya, 72.

Bibliography

Faust, Goethe. "I'd Sell My Soul to Publish a Book About Candy. In *Dubious Arguments*. Chicago: Arguers Anonymous Press, 1998.

Onya, Liz. *Let's Eat Some More*. New York: Glutton & Sons, 1994.

Kaloreese, Lotta. "Men Who Would Be Children." In *Experiments in Chocolate*. Edited by Russell Upsom Grubb. Pennsylvania: Bar Press, 1991.

Mush, Ima. *Notes on a Sentimental Life*. Hawaii: Soft Hearts & Company, 1993.

Phat, Hy. "The Life I Could Have Had: Plain Chocolate and the Repressed." In *Watchamacallit and Aphasia: An Introduction to Chocolate and Mental Health*. Edited by Roland Butter. Arizona: Bench Press, 1992.

Schmidt, I. *Candy Bars And Personality: There's No Connection*. New York: Skeptics & Co., 1988.

Rich, Tu. *Peanuts And Machismo: I Know They Are Connected*. Texas: Men Don't Press, 1993.

Swiss, Miss. *The Mousse Inquiries*. Switzerland: Braids & Company, 1962.

Whipt, I. M. "An Important Study." *Nougat Quarterly,* 103 (1987), 12–34.

Common Research Paper Pitfalls

Getting Bogged Down in an Organizational Swamp

The organizing process may take you quite a while, and there is the temptation to say to yourself, "I've been working on this paper organization for four hours and I haven't written a thing! This is awful!" Relax. Thinking through your paper is an important step of writing.

Nonetheless, don't get caught in the endless note-taking trap. A pleasant rule of thumb: the length of your notes should not exceed the length of your paper. If you find yourself buying a second package of 100 index cards, you've gone overboard; reign yourself in, organize the cards, and start writing.

Writing Before the Research Is Done

Finish your research before you start writing, because you never know if something you find will prove your thesis wrong or right. The research process helps you know what you want to write. Writing before your research is finished is like constructing a building before the blueprint has been drawn.

Procrastinating

With an organized outlook and meticulous research you can write a term paper in less time than you might think. Nevertheless, you should still allow yourself at least one week for every five pages. Trying to write the paper in one night will, in most cases, ensure that you produce a paper that is poorly written and conceptually crippled. You've probably heard of the all-nighter, as in, "I stayed up all night and wrote the whole paper in five hours and then I got an A." For some people, that may be possible, but for most of us, it leads only to incoherent, sloppy writing. If you are the type to procrastinate, set up a written schedule giving yourself due dates for your research, your outlines, your first five pages, etc. Then give it to someone who you trust will bug you enough to remind you but not enough so you will never forgive her.

Striving for Perfection

"What?" you say, "Perfection a pitfall?"

Here's the situation: If you try to make every sentence that you write perfect as you write it, the odds are that you will never get your paper written. You will have the opportunity to edit your paper later. The purpose of the paper is to present your thesis and your research, not to write a literary masterpiece. Get your paper written in rough draft and *then* attempt perfection, or you will end up writing the first sentence for the rest of your life.

Plagiarism

Don't take credit for someone else's work, fake footnotes, or fake research. Your instructor will be able to discern original work from plagiarized work, and you will have to face the consequences.

Focusing on Quantity Over Quality

It is tempting, sometimes, to ramble on for pages and pages because you believe your paper has to achieve a certain length. Say what you mean to say and no more; any unnecessary sentences will only weaken your paper. Your paper should be long enough to cover your topic, and once you have covered it, finish. Pieces that don't belong will stick out and destabilize the structure you have invested so much time in building.

Formatting and Citations

Since term papers are all about research, you must indicate the sources of your research within your paper. This is done with footnotes (or endnotes), references within the text, and a bibliography or works cited page. Follow the style guide specified by your instructor. The main ones are MLA, APA, and Chicago.

There are some rules to follow when including references within a paper.

Quotations

Any quotation you use in your paper should be copied exactly as it appears in the original source and cited appropriately. If you must shorten a quotation, indicate that sections were removed by using the ellipses, those three dots ". . ." which translate to "Something has been omitted here."

Quotations of fewer than four typed lines should be placed within quotation marks and introduced by a comma or a colon. Quotations of four typed lines or longer are also introduced by a comma or a colon, but are set off from the text by triple spacing, and indented five lines on either side; they can also be single-spaced.

Footnotes and Endnotes

They are ordered references indicated by a superscript number after a paraphrase or quotation that is not your own.[10] These references should be used only when necessary. Useless quotes used to pad the length will be spotted, and notes that have been fractured to provide a higher number of notes will weaken your writing. Footnotes are written at the bottom of the page on which the reference appears, endnotes are given on a separate page at the end of the paper.

---

[10] It looks just like this.

Footnotes and endnotes serve the same purpose; the format you use depends on your teacher's preference.

In the body of your paper:

> The difference between owning a dog and owning a cat is simple: "dogs have masters; cats have staff."[1]

Let's say you're following Chicago style. The footnote would look like this:

[1] Kitty Lovah, "Cats Rule and Dogs Drool," in *The Ascendant Feline* (New York: Random Place, 1998), 61.

If you continue with references to the same book, you can repeat the author's last name and show the new page.

[2] Lovah, 117–118.

If you have used two different books by the same author, you can repeat the author's last name, and the title or an abbreviation of the title, and then the page number(s). Like this:

[3] Lovah, *Canine Subordination,* 56.

There are endless variations on note format, for articles in periodicals, books with multiple authors, and so on. The basic rule is that the author's name is given first; the book title is italicized; an article or section of a book is put in quotation marks; and the publication information is given.

References Within Text

These are used only in papers with very few references. Basically, include all the information you would have written in the footnote, as we just did.

Bibliography

A **bibliography** is a list of all the works used in compiling a research paper. If you have used a book or article for information, it belongs in your bibliography, even if you have not directly cited it. Do not list books you did not use, no matter how fancy you want to appear. If you have used footnotes or endnotes, you should list the works in alphabetical order without numbers. If you have used references within the text, number your entries.

Bibliographical entries are constructed differently from footnotes. Here is what a bibliography should look like, again using Chicago style.

Lebowitz, Fran. *Social Studies.* New York: Random House, 1977.

Title

Don't underline, capitalize, or do anything else fancy to the title of your research paper. You can have a title page if you want one, but it is not necessary.

Page Numbers

Do not count the title page, if you include one, in the page count. The page count starts on the first page, but you don't write down the page number until the second page. This is because we assume the reader knows that the first page he is reading is, in fact, the first page.

Italics and Quotation Marks

Titles of books, plays, and long poems get italics. If you have no italics, underline. Titles of shorter pieces get put in quotation marks.

In Conclusion...

Research papers aren't so terrible; they just call for a detailed plan of attack and a structured schedule. Writing a research paper is much like writing any other academic or non-personal essay. If you ever get stuck and don't know what to write next, ask yourself, "What am I trying to say?" and write that down. That is the surest way to clear, direct communication through writing.

Recommended Reading

These books are not generally fun to read, except *The Elements of Style*, but they contain useful information for writing research papers.

Guide to Reference Books, American Library Association.

MLA Handbook for Writers of Research Papers, Theses, and Dissertations, Modern Language Association.

William Strunk and E. B. White, *The Elements of Style*, Macmillan.

CHAPTER 8

Professional Letters

Writing for Professional Situations

There will be a time in your life when you must write some sort of professional letter or email. This may be in connection with a job or a request for a recommendation, but the time will come. This chapter prepares you for writing in business situations using a few simple steps.

Steps for Writing a Professional Letter

The basic template for a professional letter is much like any other letter: it needs an introduction (in this case, a salutation, in which you greet the recipient and introduce yourself), a body, and a closing and sign-off. A letter you will be proud of, like any other piece of writing, requires multiple drafts as well as a few steps. Here's our approach to professional letter writing.

Step 1: Know Your Purpose

The first thing you want to get straight is deciding exactly what you want to say.

> Duncan is applying for a job and needs to include a cover letter along with his resume. He has met the person in charge of hiring, and wants both to remind her of their meeting, and sound warm, witty, and competent. He writes down on his notepad:
>
> > I know you from the Texas conference on UFOs, please give me this job—I'm good at it, I have experience, I am eager to work for you. I'm not desperate either.

Step 2: Write a First Draft

Clarify your intent, and put your notes in letter form. Write freely and easily; there will be an opportunity to edit later. Try to keep your tone restrained and professional, and bear your audience in mind.

Step 3: Edit

Take a look at the original version of Duncan's letter on the next page. When editing the letter, the goal is to make sure the main ideas are clearly expressed. Also, since this is a letter for a prospective employer, it should be no more than one page in length.

After reviewing the original, take a look at our edited version that follows.

Original Version

Dear Ms. Hankshaw,

Maybe you remember me from last year's conference on aliens. I am Duncan Bock and I ran the booth on the Martian, friend or foe? I am enclosing my resume to be considered for the position of assistant commander in charge of alien visitors in your alien welcoming army.

I look forward to hearing from you.

Love, Duncan

Edited Version

expand on the meeting to jog her memory

Dear Ms. Hankshaw,

Maybe you remember me from last year's conference on aliens. I am Duncan Bock and I ran the booth on the Martian, friend or foe? I am enclosing my resume to be considered for the position of assistant commander in charge of alien visitors in your alien welcoming army.

I look forward to hearing from you.

Love, Duncan

list credentials

punctuation

capitalize title

why?

not her responsibility

Enclosures?

Step 4: Write the Final Draft

The last step is to put the letter in its final form. If at all possible, try to find someone else to read the letter to point out any errors. Pay close attention to matters of form because the look of a business letter is just as important as its content. Check carefully for mistakes, whether in grammar, format, or tone. Notice on this final draft the changes that were made to accommodate edits for tone and style on the previous drafts.

Duncan Smith
123 Conspiracy Lane
New York 11111

ADDRESS

June 5, 2018

Ms. Hankshaw
Commander of Forces
Aliens Are Coming Soon, Inc.
2435 Outuvmy Way
Los Angeles, California 90210

Dear Ms. Hankshaw: **SALUTATION**

I had the privilege of meeting you at the 2017 Conference on Alien Life where I ran the booth, "Martian: Friend or Foe?" I enjoyed speaking with you regarding the future of our extraterrestrial communications systems. Your project and the above-mentioned position sound extremely exciting. I look forward to finding out more about both.

BODY

I am writing to be considered for the position of assistant commander in charge of welcoming alien visitors. I have worked welcoming various extraterrestrial visitors all over California and the southwest, receiving the prestigious E.T. award, among others. I have enjoyed this work and the people and aliens I have been privileged to encounter.

I would be delighted if you would review my enclosed resume and consider me for this position. I hope to hear from you soon.

Sincerely, **CLOSING**

Duncan Smith

Duncan Smith
Enc. Resume **ENCLOSURES**

The Strongly Worded Letter

Let's say you're in a situation in which you need to write a letter addressing a concern or voicing a complaint. Maybe you purchased a malfunctioning product, or your cable company overcharged you, or you need to voice your discontent to your landlord. While many situations may call for a phone call or in-person conversation, sometimes a letter or email is more appropriate. In such cases, here's a basic format you can use to get your point across and your concerns heard while still maintaining a calm, levelheaded tone.

Strongly Worded Letter Format

Here's the general template:

Salutation and Opening

Identify yourself and to whose attention you wish to address your concerns.

Body

Describe the unfortunate event the letter refers to in the most specific terms possible.

Closing

Indicate how you want the company or person to redress your grievances.

Writing the Strongly Worded Letter

Step 1: Identify Yourself and Your Reason for Writing

To begin, you must clearly state your concern or issue. You should be firm but polite. No matter what your personal feelings are, you should never resort to obscenities or name calling. Remember that the person who ends up reading your email is unlikely to be the person who directly caused the issue you are complaining about (in the case of an extra charge on your cable bill, for example).

Step 2: Write a Rough Draft

Compile your notes into a rough first draft. You should follow the format given earlier in this chapter. Then, use an appropriate amount of detail to describe your complaint or issue and any necessary background the recipient might need. Be sure to describe the situation in a clear chronological order to avoid any confusion.

Step 3: Edit

Edit the following rough draft a strongly worded letter with the goal of making it more restrained, polite, and clear. Compare the original with our edited version that follows.

Mr. Smith:

Two months ago I sent you a letter detailing the problems I was experiencing with my rotating turkey in my doll house oven on my doll house model #25143. I informed you that I had received in return a letter from your company noting that I would *not* be compensated for my troubles. When I discussed that letter with you on the phone you said, "It's a mistake. The department made a mistake and about 6 million customers got one of those letters. Just send it to me and I'll take care of it. I will get you registered as a customer with a complaint and you will be reimbursed for your turkey, as well as your pain and suffering." I sent it to you and assumed that there would be no problem.

Two weeks ago, January 24, I received another notice that I would not be receiving reimbursement for my pain and suffering, and that I owed for the repair to the turkey as well as interest on the repair bill. I then called your office on Monday, January 24. No response. I called Tuesday, Wednesday, etc. On Friday at 5 P.M. I got a message from you, but of course I was unable to reach you as your office had closed. I called every day of the next week. I got one more call from you saying you would be reachable on Wednesday February 2, in the morning. I called at 8:55 A.M. and 9:30 A.M. Either no one answered or I was told you were not in. I called again every day, sometimes twice a day, and was told you were out in "the field."

That may in fact be the case, but there are phones in other places. I was given to understand that you were dealing with important clients. I am an important client too. While I was not pleased that my rotating turkey did not function, I am even more offended by the way you have responded to my attempts to address the situation. I paid you $200 for the doll house and a lifetime of servicing and you did it poorly. You rude idiot, I will not be treated this way!! You can forget any other business from me you idiotic dolt. I expect you to pay the $22.69 in interest I was assessed, and I expect you to return my initial payment of $200 which, I think you will agree, you did not earn.

Edited First Draft

Mr. Smith:

Two months ago I sent you a letter detailing the problems I was experiencing with ~~my~~ rotating turkey in ~~my~~ doll
house oven on ~~my~~ doll house model #25143. I informed
you that I had received ~~in return~~ a letter from your company
noting that I would ~~not~~ be compensated for my troubles.
When I discussed that letter with you on the phone, you
said, "It's a mistake. The department made a mistake and
about 6 million customers got one of those letters. Just
send it to me and I'll take care of it. I will get you registered
as a customer with a complaint and you will be reimbursed
for your turkey, as well as your pain and suffering." I sent
it to you and assumed that there would be no problem.

redundant

unnecessary

o italics

Two weeks ago, January 24, I received another notice
that I would not be receiving reimbursement for my pain
and suffering, and that I owed for the repair to the turkey
as well as interest on the repair bill. I then called your
office on Monday, January 24. No response. I called Tuesday, Wednesday, etc. On Friday at 5 P.M. I got a message
from you, but of course I was unable to reach you as your
office had closed. I called every day of the next week. I
got one more call from you saying you would be reachable on Wednesday February 2, in the morning. I called at
8:55 A.M. and 9:30 A.M. ~~Either~~ no one answered ~~or~~ I was
told you were not in. I called again every day, sometimes
twice a day, and was told you were out in "the field."

Both happened

That may in fact be the case, but there are phones in
other places. ~~I was given to understand~~ that you were dealing with important clients. I am an important client too.
While I was not pleased that my rotating turkey did not
function, I am even more offended by the way you have
responded to my attempts to address the situation. I paid
you $200 for the doll house and a lifetime of servicing
and you did it poorly. You rude idiot, I will not be treated
this way!! You can forget any other business from me, you
idiotic dolt. I expect you to pay the $22.69 in interest I
was assessed, and I expect you to return my initial payment of $200 which, I think you will agree, you did not
earn.

It was my understanding [margin note]

calm down
detail
rational
retaliation [margin notes]

he did not
do it
at all [margin note]

not just him,
the whole
company [margin note]

Step 4: Write the Final Draft

The final draft of a letter must be as perfect as you can make it.
Be sure to fix any typos, spelling errors, or grammatical mistakes—
remember that such mistakes can be distracting and even discredit
you to the recipient. The final version should be firm but polite and
respectful. You should absolutely refrain from using profanity or
insulting anyone, as this is unethical and will ultimately do you a
disservice. Even when you feel you have been wronged, it's important to be remain civil and calm. The final draft is written in the
form of a business letter; if this is an email, you would not include
the mailing addresses as shown.

Final Draft

Connie Smith

123 Main Street

New York, NY 11111

February 7, 2018

Otto Smith

Babyface Cute Doll Houses, Inc.

456 Main Avenue

New York, NY 22222

Dear Mr. Smith,

Two months ago I sent you a letter detailing the problems I was experiencing with the rotating turkey in my doll house oven on doll house model #25143. I informed you that I had received a letter from your company noting that I would not be compensated for my troubles. When I discussed that letter with you on the phone you said, "It's a mistake. The department made a mistake and about 6 million customers got one of those letters. Just send it to me and I'll take care of it. I will get you registered as a customer with a complaint and you will be reimbursed for your turkey, as well as your pain and suffering." I sent it to you and assumed you would take care of the problem.

Two weeks ago, January 24, I received another notice that I would not receive reimbursement for my pain and suffering, and that I owed for the repair to the turkey as well as interest on the repair bill. I then called your office on Monday, January 24. I received no response. I called Tuesday, Wednesday, etc. Once again, I received no response. On Friday at 5 P.M. I got a message from you, but I was unable to reach you as your office had closed. I called every day of the next week. I got one more call from you saying you would be reachable on Wednesday, February 2, in the morning. I called at 8:55 A.M. and 9:30 A.M. First, no one answered, then I was told you were not in. I called again every day, sometimes twice a day, and was told you were out in "the field."

That may in fact be the case, but there are phones in other places. It was my understanding that you were dealing with important clients, but I feel I am an important client too. While I was not pleased that my rotating turkey did not function, I am even more dissatisfied with the way you have responded to my attempts to address the situation. I paid you $200 for a functioning doll house and a lifetime of servicing, and received neither. Kindly return my $200 payment and further reimburse me for the $22.89 in interest that I was mistakenly charged. I thank you in advance for your prompt attention to this matter.

Regards,

Connie Smith

Notice that in the final version of the letter Connie expresses her concerns while maintaining a professional tone. She also informs Mr. Smith of the ways he can fix the problems. These are the goals of any outraged letter.

Common Pitfalls in Letter Writing

Using "Gentlemen"

Beginning a letter with "Gentlemen," which assumes that the recipient is a man, is inappropriate and will make you appear very out of touch and perhaps insensitive. If you do not know whether your recipient is a man or woman, it is best to use an opening that is non-gender-specific, such as "To whom it may concern."

Signing Off with "Love"

This seems obvious, but the word "love" does not have any place in a professional letter. Unless you're writing to a family member or close friend, leave "love" out of it and stick with a neutral closing, such as "Sincerely," or "Regards."

You should not be overly familiar or make personal comments. This will only alienate your reader and make them uncomfortable. Maintain a reserved tone.

Rambling

In general, professional letters of any kind should be concise and to the point. This especially goes for letters in which you are applying for a job or other position. Believe us when we tell you that your recipient will appreciate brevity.

Using Profanity or Strong Language

Under no circumstances should you use profanity, name-calling, or insults in a letter, no matter how angry you may be. If your letter is intended to voice a complaint, you should calmly and matter-of-factly explain your issue; this will allow your concerns to be taken more seriously. When you resort to expletives and an angry tone, your recipient will be turned off right away and will be less inclined to address your concerns and give you the outcome you want.

Formatting and Style for Professional Letters

- Include both your name and address and the recipient's name and address. Your name should be at the top of the page, flush with the right margin, along with the date. The recipient's information should be below your name, flush with the left margin.

- After the recipient's information, insert a double space (hit ENTER or RETURN twice) and then begin your salutation: *Dear Ms./Mr. [Name],* followed by a comma or colon (either is fine).

- You can either indent paragraphs or include double spaces between paragraphs. Professional letters generally use the double space.

- Your sign-off should be on the lower left of the letter, followed by a comma, then two double spaces are left empty. This is so you can sign your name with an appropriate flourish. After the signature space, also on the lower left, you should type out your name, in full.

- If necessary, extra markings can alert the recipient of the letter to any enclosures (Enc.) or other copies sent that may be of interest to them (cc: Mr. Ed). The "cc" stands for the long-ago carbon copy, and should be marked if you want the recipient to know you have sent the same letter to his boss, or someone else within the same company.

A Few Words About Email

As society becomes increasingly fast-paced, it is often standard practice for business and professional correspondence to take place via email. Regardless of *how* a professional letter gets from the writer to the reader, however, the rules and procedures outlined in this chapter apply. Don't be lulled into a false sense of informality by the ease with which you can send a message through cyberspace! Below are a few guidelines that apply specifically to email correspondence:

1. Distinguish between informal and formal exchanges.

Typing up one of the elegant-looking letters we've dealt with in this chapter and snail mailing it has a ceremonious air. Consequently, we're less likely to make the mistake of writing in an inappropriately familiar way. This is, unfortunately, not the case with email. One moment we might email our best friend with a hilariously edgy joke, and the next moment email a prospective business client about an important meeting. Just because the individual you're emailing is friendly and cordial does not mean that anything goes! If you stop and think before hitting the "send" button, chances are you'll make the right call. Informal emails among family and friends can be whatever you want them to be. The remaining rules will therefore refer to emails sent in a business or professional context.

2. Include a subject line that is accurate and helpful.

The person to whom you're sending the email may have hundreds of messages to sift through while searching for your project proposal, memorandum, etc. Including a subject line that clearly identifies the topic will help both you and the recipient tremendously. Don't simply reply to the last email you received from someone without editing the subject if you're addressing a different topic. Moreover, whenever possible try to send a separate email for each topic you cover. Your boss is unlikely to remember that your email entitled "Agenda for Staff Meeting" also included a request for time off.

3.   Organize email content just as you would in any other letter.

While most people organize traditional business letters according to a standard format, they often feel welcome to ramble on in their emails. Just like any other piece of writing, an email should be divided logically into discrete paragraphs. The fact that you're communicating electronically doesn't excuse laziness. The easier you make it for the reader to follow your train of thought, the more receptive he will be to your ideas.

4.   Avoid using emojis, emoticons, unusual fonts, colored backgrounds, and the like.

This sort of falls under the first guideline of "keep formal correspondence formal," but it's worth mentioning nonetheless. Some business settings and contexts require stricter decorum than others. When in doubt, however, err on the side of keeping professional exchanges strictly professional.

5.   Double-check (or even triple-check) emails before you send them.

When corresponding by regular mail, you're much less likely to send a letter to the wrong person, enclose an incorrect document, or inadvertently omit half the text (unless you're particularly absent-minded)! With email, however, it's alarmingly easy to mistakenly send your vacation photos to a prospective employer instead of your resume, or to send that memo complaining about your obnoxious new client to the client! Never hit "send" until you're certain everything is in order.

6.   Never assume that your emails are private.

Many employees have learned this the hard way. Once you send an email, where it goes and who sees it are no longer within your control. Be wary!

7. Don't reply too quickly.

Before immediately responding to an email, make sure that you've thought the matter through. The ability to reply instantaneously can cause you to look foolish if your email is ill-conceived or incoherent. Moreover, emailing impulsively or when highly emotional rarely ends well.

8. Don't be blunt.

All good writing is succinct. However, that does not mean that the rules of common courtesy do not apply. Few people would send a traditional letter consisting of one line such as "where is my money, Mr. Babyface?" Yet sometimes we neglect the niceties when communicating over the Internet. Unless you've been exchanging multiple emails with someone over a short period, your email should include a greeting, a pleasant remark or two, and a word of closure. Simply approach others as you would like to be approached, and you won't go wrong here.

9. Never rely on spellcheck!

This last one cannot be emphasized enough. While computers are becoming more sophisticated, they still lack the ability to proof-read as a human being would. Only you know what you *meant* to write, and errors in word usage often go undetected by machines. Computer functions designed to check grammar and spelling should be used only *after* you've double-checked your writing yourself.

In Conclusion...

Though many believe letters have gone the way of the horse and carriage, a well-written letter can have more impact than a million phone messages. Your letter will allow you to present yourself clearly and cogently, and if you take the time to craft and check it, can display your eloquence far better than a conversation. So practice; this skill will serve you well your entire life.

Recommended Reading

Some of these books contain letters and some contain instructions on how to write letters. All promote the letter as a powerful tool. See what you can learn from them.

Alfred Stuart Nuyers, *Letters for All Occasions,* Harper Perennial.

Rainer Maria Rilke, *Letters to a Young Poet,* Vintage Press.

John Stiker and Andrew Shapiro, *Superthreats: How to Sound Like a Lawyer and Get Your Rights on Your Own,* Rawson Associates.

William Strunk and E. B. White, *The Elements of Style,* Macmillan.

CHAPTER 9

Lab Reports

Why Write a Lab Report?

Why does your teacher want you to write a lab report detailing your experiment anyway? You may think it is a sneaky way to prove that you have actually done the experiment. If, however, you take a moment to consider the parts of a lab report, you will see a larger truth emerge. You write a lab report so you can indicate your personal thought process as it relates to the experiment or study performed. For instance, you might have dissolved aspirin until it became wintergreen oil, but it makes no difference if you did this or exploded marshmallows in the microwave unless you understand *why* you did it, and what the results mean.

Experimentation is often misunderstood. You may have heard comments like, "The experiment was unsuccessful; we have failed in our mission." Don't worry about "failing." An experiment is an attempt to discover how something will react in a given situation. Since you will always discover something, the experiment is always a success, even if what you find out annoys you. You write a lab report to say what you thought you might observe, then what you did observe, and what you think it all means. So whether you notice, like Sir Alexander Fleming, that there's a tiny mold that's destroying all the other stuff in your petri dish, or you notice that when you add substance A to substance B not a darn thing happens, you have something to write down and a great lab report to deliver. As long as you know why you were performing the experiment in the first place, and what the results show you, your experiment is a success.

Lab Report Format

While individual teachers or professors may have particular specifications, the general format for a lab report is as follows:

Purpose of Experiment

This is the first paragraph of your report, and it contains exactly what it says. Why are you doing your experiment? What do you hope to find or discover? The answer to these questions is your purpose, which gives the experiment and your observations a context.

Materials

List the materials and their amounts in case someone wants to replicate your findings.

Step-by-Step Process of Experiment

Write exactly what happened in chronological order: what actions you performed and what you observed to follow from these actions. When you have the opportunity, illustrate your process with detailed drawings. Some teachers will require that this section be laid out numerically as in step one, step two, and so on. Others will prefer that you present this section in paragraph form.

Outcome, Discussion of Outcome, Conclusions

Here is where the purpose of your experiment and the observations come together. If the results were as you expected, say what that means and why the results are as they are. If the results were other than what you had expected, explain why, if you can. If you don't know why you achieved the results you did, offer some hypotheses. Conclude with a statement indicating how this experiment and the results you observed furthered your understanding of what you studied.

Make sure you check this outline with the requirements of your class. Most lab reports will include at least these basic requirements.

Writing the Lab Report

Step 1: Decide on the Experiment and Read Any Background Material

Usually, you write a lab report based on experiments you perform in school. If you have to select your own experiment, make it something you want to explore. Can too many fish sticks really make you sick? Which is better, Coke or Pepsi? What really happens when you put marshmallows in the microwave?

Nell, a brilliant and enterprising young scientist, will conduct her experiment at home because she is extremely motivated and was told she can earn extra credit by doing so. She has always had the feeling that her dogs understand what she says to them; now is her opportunity to test this out. She will attempt to discover whether dogs understand what people are saying. She has an eerie feeling they do, and she has planned an experiment to help her prove it. She has three dogs: Geoff, Almon, and Mike. She is going to use Geoff as the "control dog." She will play Almon the same calming story every day, she will play Mike sad dog stories every day for five days, and she will simply observe Geoff at the same time each day, without playing any story. She will record the dogs' responses daily.

If your experiment is assigned in class, you will probably be assigned a chapter to read. Read it! If you don't know why you are conducting the experiment, you will have a tough time grasping the concepts, staying interested, and writing a decent lab report.

Step 2: Assemble Your List of Materials

When you are performing experiments, orderliness is extremely important. If you are not exact, your results will be suspect, so try to be careful. Write down everything you have set up before you start your process. Be sure to include any exact measurements for mass, weight, or volume, for example.

Nell takes out her notebook and writes down the following:

Almon (Chocolate Lab)
Mike (Lovable mutt)
Geoff (Spaniel)
Recordings (audiobooks) of happy stories for dogs
Recordings (audiobooks) of sad stories for dogs
Phone, tablet, or laptop to play the recordings
Notebook for observations
Special closed-off room for observations

Step 3: Perform Your Experiment While Taking Notes

To write a complete lab report you must make accurate observations *while* you perform your experiment, even if that means just writing down, "The mixture is turning blue and fizzy, it is overflowing out of the beaker, the desk has caught fire, must go." Be as descriptive and accurate as possible; these notes will form the bulk of your report.

Nell marks Day 1 in her notebook, and takes Almon into the observation room where she plays a recording of *See Spot Run*. She marks down everything Almon does. She then removes Almon and repeats the process for Mike, playing him the same story, and then takes Geoff into the room and observes him *without* playing a story. On Day 2, she plays *See Spot Run* for Almon, one of the unhappy dog stories for Mike, and again no story for Geoff. For the next five days, she plays *See Spot Run* for Almon, a different sad dog story for Mike, and no story at all for Geoff, noting that Mike seems to get happier and happier, and Almon seems to become more agitated. She marks down these observations and ponders them.

Step 4: Write It

Once you have performed the experiment and taken notes, writing your lab report will be straightforward. Follow this format: write the introduction and purpose of the experiment, then the materials, then the observations, and finally the conclusions and any commentary.

DOGS AND LITERATURE

by Nell

The purpose of my experiment was to test whether my dogs can, as I believe they can, understand what I say to them. I tested this theory by recording three dogs' responses to calming texts read aloud, both calming and upsetting texts read aloud, and no texts read. Three dogs, Geoff, Almon, and Mike were my subjects. Geoff was not read to at all, Almon was read a soothing dog text—*See Spot Run*—and Mike was read a variety of sad dog texts. All the dogs' reactions were monitored to determine whether they corresponded to the text read. The hypothesis was that if the dogs understood what they heard, they should have been fine and relaxed throughout the calm text, upset by the upsetting text, and unaffected by the absence of any text.

SUBJECTS AND MATERIALS

Mike—Lovable mutt, aged 2 years, weight 15 pounds.
Almon—Chocolate Lab, aged 2 years, 6 months, weight 60 pounds.
Geoff—Spaniel, aged 3 years, weight 21 pounds.
Recordings of:
- *See Spot Run*—happy dog story
- *Cujo*—sad dog story
- *Champ, Gallant Collie*—sad dog story
- *The Spotted Dotted Puppy*—sad dog story
- *101 Dalmatians*—sad dog story (ultimate triumph excluded)

Figure 1

Almon   Mike   Geoff

PROCEDURE

Day 1

Almon: Played *See Spot Run*, a happy dog story, for 15 minutes. Almon walked around room for 4 minutes, scratched himself for 7.5 minutes, yawned 4 times, wagged his tail for 3.5 minutes.

Mike: Played *See Spot Run* for 15 minutes. Received same general responses, 8 minutes of scratching, 5 minutes of walking around room sniffing things, 3 minutes of tail-wagging, and 5 yawns.

Geoff: Played no story recording and did not speak to him. He napped for 15 minutes.

Day 2

Almon: Played *See Spot Run* for Almon for 15 minutes. Almon walked and sniffed for 5 minutes this time, scratched himself for 6 minutes, yawned twice, and stood and wagged his tail for 4 minutes.

Mike: Played *Spotted Dotted Puppy,* a story of conformity and abandonment in the animal world. Mike trotted around the room for 8 minutes, wagging his tail, then scratched himself for the remainder of the time (7 minutes). Yawned 3 times.

Geoff: Played no story recording and did not speak to him. He napped for 15 minutes.

Day 3

Almon: Played *See Spot Run* for Almon for 15 minutes. Almon walked around the room for 2 minutes, and then stopped and started growling at the tape recorder during the section in which Jane sees Spot run. The growling continued for 6 minutes, after which Almon started yelping and whining, for 5 minutes. The final 2 minutes Almon alternately scratched his ear vigorously and whined.

Mike: Played *Champ, Gallant Collie.* Watched closely, particularly the section in which Champ is attacked by a mountain lion and almost loses an entire herd of sheep. Mike walked and sniffed for 7 minutes, yawned 3 times, wagged his tail for 6 minutes, and scratched himself for 3 minutes.

Geoff: Played no story recording and did not speak to him. He napped, woke up after 8.5 minutes, yawned, and returned to napping.

Day 4

Almon: [Note: Almon seemed reluctant to enter the room today.] Played *See Spot Run* for Almon for 15 minutes. There was no tail-wagging at all for the second day in a row, and a repetition of yesterday's growling episode lasted for 11 minutes. The final 4 minutes consisted of Almon lying on the floor and shuffling along on his front paws, whining.

Mike: Played Mike *Cujo* for 15 minutes. Paid particular attention to the section in which Cujo suffers a tragic accident. Mike trotted around the room for 8 minutes, wagging his tail, then scratched himself for the remainder of the time (7 minutes). Yawned 3 times.

Geoff: Played no story recording and did not speak to him. He napped for 15 minutes.

Day 5

Almon: Almon was highly reluctant to enter the listening room today. Played *See Spot Run* for Almon for 15 minutes. Almon spent the entire 15 minutes howling.

Mike: Played Mike *101 Dalmatians,* the excerpt in which Cruella de Vil outlines her plans to make a coat from puppy skins. Mike sniffed and walked for 5.5 minutes, sat and wagged his tail for 5.5 minutes, and rested for 4 minutes, yawning 3 times.

Geoff: Played no story recording and did not speak to him. He napped for 15 minutes.

<u>CONCLUSION</u>

The results were not exactly what I had anticipated. I hypothesized that hearing the upsetting stories would affect Mike in such a way that he expressed anxiety, yet he remained essentially the same day after day. Almon, on the other hand, whom I expected to remain the same, as he was being read the same story day after day, expressed extreme anxiety. Geoff remained the same every day; from this I can infer that no outside influence (such as a storm coming or a change in diet) accounted for the responses of Almon and Mike. I conclude from this that dogs probably don't understand the words they are being read. However, I believe this experiment justifies further research as to whether dogs recognize repetitive sounds, as was so clearly demonstrated by Almon's response to *See Spot Run* day after day. Thus, though I cannot say I have proven that dogs understand English, I can say that I have opened the door to future scientific inquiry.

Step 5: Proofread

Check back to see that all illustrations and charts are correctly numbered and easily understood. Check for spelling, grammar, and punctuation. Also make sure that the purpose of the experiment is clear, and that your conclusion is well-founded.

Common Lab Report Pitfalls

Overly Technical Language

Many students and novice science writers fall into the trap of thinking that science writing must be loaded with technical terms. Not so! Like all other writing, science writing is meant to be read. And you can bet your instructor will want to read a report that is clear and to the point.

Not Having a Unique Perspective

Finding out what happens when you pour sulfuric acid over a candy bar, or whatever your particular experiment is, can be really interesting. That's why scientists of old started all of this: they wanted to know what would happen. Sure, everyone else in the class might be doing the same experiment, but your perspective and interest in the result are your own. If you show interest in your subject and experiment, your lap report will be more engaging for the reader.

Lack of Visuals

The great thing about lab reports is that, unlike most academic writing, you can insert figures and diagrams. Don't let this opportunity escape you!

Lack of Purpose

The point of a lab report is to present your experiment and why you performed it; if you do not know your purpose or if you are unable to convey your purpose in writing, your lab report will make little sense. There are some who write a lab report without this crucial knowledge, so their lab reports become an odd listing of things they did in science class that day, without any understanding of why they did them. Don't let this happen. Start by looking at the material your teacher or professor gave you with your lab assignment. Why do they want you to do the assignment? If you don't know, ask questions.

Then create an outline, including a description of the experiment and why you performed it. Did everything happen the way you had expected or predicted it would? If not, why do you think that might be? Know what you what you want to say before you start writing, and your lab report will be much easier to write.

Format and Style for Lab Reports

Format

Some lab reports accept a numbered list of steps rather than a sentence-by-sentence paragraph for the procedures section. Follow any directions provided by your teacher or professor regarding format.

Rough Drafts

Generally, lab reports do not go through the rigorous draft process to which essays and research papers are subjected. Before you hand your lab report in, you should still proofread it for any possible errors, but the full-fledged stylistic editing process is generally used more on scientific research papers, which are formatted like regular research papers and are edited as such.

Title

Always include a title page. It gives you the opportunity to clearly lay out your topic right away as well as use visual aids.

References

Unless your instructor requests one, there is generally no need to supply a bibliography or any other list of sources. If you do use a quote from someone's work, provide the name of the author and the title in parentheses within the report.

In Conclusion...

Lab reports benefit from lucid prose—that is, clear, organized writing. Your reports will shine when you understand your experiment before you begin writing and express what you mean as clearly as you can.

Recommended Reading

The following books discuss science in a clear exciting way understandable to the non-scientist. Read, enjoy, and emulate.

Isaac Asimov, *Isaac Asimov's Guide to Earth and Space,* Fawcett.

Rachel Carson, *Silent Spring,* Houghton Mifflin.

James Gleick, *Chaos,* The Penguin Group.

Stephen Jay Gould, *Bully for Brontosaurus,* Norton.

David MacCauley, *The Way Things Work,* Houghton Mifflin.

John McPhee, *In Suspect Terrain,* The Noonday Press.

Lewis Thomas, *The Lives of a Cell,* Bantam Books.

Lewis Thomas, *The Medusa and the Snail,* G.K. Hall and Company.

CHAPTER 10

Project Proposals

So You Need to Write a Project Proposal...

Maybe you need to present a business idea to your boss. Or maybe you are applying for a grant and need to outline your project to demonstrate how worthwhile and why it deserves funding. A **project proposal** is a written description of your project along with a rationale for why it should be undertaken or funded.

Whatever the occasion for your proposal, don't panic. The process of writing a project proposal is relatively straightforward; all you need is a good idea, a plan, and enthusiasm.

Project Proposal Format

Introduction

The introduction should state how your idea came to be. If your project is to satisfy some hole in the array of products in the world, here you can write, "It was always clear to me that there were not enough different types of cookie jars in the world." Then, describe your project and how it will address that need.

Body of Proposal

This section will always be divided into three parts.

---

1. *The Idea:* A summary of your idea

2. *Your Plan:* What you will do once your project is approved

3. *You:* Your particular qualifications for the task or project

---

While not absolutely necessary, you may want to itemize the costs and other financial needs of your project in this section as well. This will show your employer or whoever is reading this proposal that you are doing your homework.

Conclusion

Wrap up your proposal with a convincing argument for why your idea is a great one, and include a graceful sign-off.

Writing the Project Proposal

Step 1: Create an Outline

You first need to organize your thoughts, and as we have discussed elsewhere in this book, the best way to do that is to write an outline. An outline for a project proposal gives you a chance to write down your idea and lay out your plan for selling it.

> Lisa and Mimi have an idea; they want someone to give them money so they can travel around the world for a few years by boat, having a wonderful time. They call this project the Sailing Sisters. They estimate they need $5 million. They want to write the proposal together, which makes it a collaborative project. Yet they have no fear; they know that if you start with a clear plan, collaborative writing can be less work and more fun than writing alone.

To begin, both Lisa and Mimi write outlines, which they will then compare and meld into one.

Lisa's Outline

I. Introduction: Why? There aren't enough women having fun out there; there is a great need for a few raise-hell women.
    A. Evidence for this, success of *Thelma and Louise*, the movie of women raising hell
    B. People's undying interest in the antics of supermodels
    C. Success of "Absolutely Fabulous," British television series in which a couple of hellions tear up the town
    D. Sailing Sisters: we want to have fun.
II. Idea: Mimi and I on a boat with plenty of money and a radio; the possibilities are endless
    A. A couple of scenarios? Mimi and I swim in the Aegean, Mimi and I disrupt a boring meeting and create an international incident, Mimi and I skydive in Venezuela.
    B. When we get the money, we buy the boat and set sail.
    C. Why us? Mimi has sailed before; we are ready for this kind of fun.
III. Costs: How much the boat, the food, etc. will cost
IV. Conclusion: How great it will be to have this need filled and how worthy a cause it is

Mimi's Outline

I. Introduction
    <u>Why?</u> There is no record of women taking a trip like this.
    <u>Idea</u>: Sailing Sisters—Lisa and I take a boat and sail and sail and sail, island to island, then write a book.

II. Idea
    A. The Plan: We outline the plan of going from island to island, starting on Martha's Vineyard, then south, then east. Give an example of the kind of entry we would write.
    B. With the money we first do research about other island-to-island boat jaunts throughout history, then buy a boat, then itinerary.
    C. Why us? We are interested in women and history and the history of travel; we can do the island-to-island thing with a historical perspective; we can write a book about it.

III. Conclusion: How worthy it would be to have this kind of travel history done by women, right now!

> Lisa and Mimi get together and compare notes. Their outlines are so different! Their ideas for the trip are so divergent! Or are they? They spend some time discussing the particulars of each of their proposals. Do they really want to make a book of this? Is it for fun or for historical importance, and is there a difference between these two goals?

This discussion and comparison of goals is of the utmost importance for anyone planning a collaborative writing project. It allows you to compare ideas and really come up with a common focus, *before* the bulk of the writing is done.

Lisa and Mimi first try to decide whether they really do want to write a book about their adventures. Mimi confesses that she included that section in her outline because she wanted to sound worthier of funding. Lisa says that, actually, they don't need to sound worthy of funding, they *are* worthy of funding. Why pretend to be scholars when they are not? They have other attributes, and their project is not about books.

Next to be decided is the perspective of the trip. Is it for fun or for history? Again, they talk about what they really want to do. They decide that what they really want is not to talk about travel but to have some fun. They ponder all of this for some time and decide to focus on the hell-raising women aspect of the trip; they want to do this to have a good time, so why shouldn't that be their strength? And, after all, they want to be honest about the funding they seek. Mimi volunteers to write the final outline for the proposal, which Lisa will then check over.

Final Outline

I.   Introduction
     <u>Why</u>: There is a great need for images of women being daring and reckless. The public is hungry for it, witness.
     A.   Success of *Thelma and Louise*, the movie of women raising hell
     B.   People's undying interest in the antics of supermodels
     C.   Success of "Absolutely Fabulous," British television series in which a couple of hellions tear up the town
          <u>Therefore</u>: We will go on a no-holds-barred ocean-going tour.

II. Plan

   Idea: We will buy a sailboat and adventure across the open seas, inspiring all who hear tell of us.

   Scenarios:

   A. Skydiving in Venezuela

   B. Swimming in the Aegean

   C. Barging into a meeting and creating an international incident

      How: With the funds we receive, we will buy a boat and go where the winds take us.

      Why us: We have the time, the inclination, and the wild-woman credentials.

III. Conclusion: It's really a great idea.

Step 2: Check Your Outline

Read your outline and determine if it gives you a clear writing plan. Do you know the gist of what you want to get across? Do you understand what you will write? If so, continue. If not, rework your outline until it fulfills these guidelines.

Step 3: Gather Your Data and Write a Rough Draft

A good project proposal is one that is based on diligent research and reflects that diligent research. If you are competing with others for a project, point out your strengths, supporting your points with hard data. If you are demonstrating a need for stuffed-crust pizza that you are going to fill, note that there were over one million calls for stuffed-crust pizza recorded by Pizza Palace.

Once you have gathered as many facts and figures as you can—by using any information source that occurs to you—you can begin writing. Writing a project proposal is much like writing a research paper. You follow your outline, paragraph by paragraph, and put together a rough draft to work from. When you are working collaboratively, you might assign one person research and the other writing. Another possibility is to assign separate sections of the outline to each person. For instance, the introduction and the idea sections might go to one person, and the conclusion and the other body paragraphs to the other. This second option can be difficult when you are putting the whole proposal together, because often people have different writing styles; putting the pieces together will require you to make the whole proposal stylistically uniform. Choose the best option based on your group's strengths and weaknesses. For example, the stronger public speaker should do the talking, and the more skilled writer should do the writing. Try to determine this division of labor ahead of time, as negotiations in the middle of writing can make an already difficult task more trying.

> Mimi and Lisa decide that Lisa will be responsible for the research, and Mimi will write the proposal, which will then be edited and revised by Lisa. Lisa goes to the library and finds books about adventuring women, women sailors, and sea-going. She calls the Motion Picture Association of America and finds out how many people went to see *Thelma and Louise.* Meanwhile, Mimi sits on the veranda, sips lemonade, and thinks of convincing images to put in her writing. When Lisa has accumulated enough facts, she gives her copious and well-organized notes to Mimi, who then goes inside to her laptop.

Step 4: Edit

Edit your proposal, aiming to make it professional, convincing, and clear. You know what to do, and if you need reminding, look back to the editing guidelines in Chapter 4.

One more time! Edit Mimi's rough draft, checking for clarity, organization, and brevity. When you're done, see if Lisa's edits agree with yours.

Rough Draft

Everyone craves adventure. Executives tucked away in offices, professors stranded in ivy covered buildings, doctors overworked in emergency rooms, parents exhausted from car-pooling; all of them dream of mountain climbing or deep-sea diving or traveling through Amazon jungles. Everyone craves adventure, but most people find it vicariously. People want images of adventurous people to inspire them, and consider how many of those executives, professors, doctors and parents are women. There is a lack of daring images of women, and people are willing to pay for them when they can find them. Consider the success of Thelma & Louise, a film about women finding adventure on the open road. Women did not go on shooting sprees, but they flocked in droves to see the movie; it was one of the seven most popular films of 1991. Yet it was the only reckless kick-butt female adventure film made over the next two years. Consider the public's interest in the antics of supermodels: "What are they doing now? What will they do next? Where are they now?" The supermodels traipse over Europe masking money, breaking hearts and painting the towns red, and people hang on their every bad-girl move. In Absolutely Fabulous, the cult hit of British television, a couple of women tear up London, leaving chaos and nail polish in their wake. How to address this need? We propose to buy a boat and take a free-wheeling ocean going tour.

We propose to buy a sturdy ocean going sail boat and adventure across the open seas. We will go from island to continent to island, taking risks and having adventures. We will swim in the jewel-like waters if the Mediterranean and scale the cliffs of Dover. What are the benefits? We will be sky-diving in Venezuela and then we will sail off to Saint Thomas. A young boy will say, "Wow. The thought of that makes me so happy I will not throw this bowl of mashed peas on the floor but will instead wait for my mother to take it from my high chair." We will be swimming in the Aegean Sea and a politician in her office will pick up her pen and say, "Gosh, the idea of them swimming makes me so thrilled I will sign this treaty ending all war everywhere." We will storm into a meeting in Portugal and everyone will talk about it for days, instead of harping on the drab details of some actor's divorce, thus sparing both the public and the actor. Aside from these benefits to the public, we will be having a wonderful time, and in doing so, will provide the world of women with role models, with an idea of how to live life on the edge and to the fullest.

We will accomplish this plan with a grant of $5,000,000. First we will buy the boat, and some necessary luggage, rations, and navigating charts. The money that remains after this will be used as spending money so we can instruct the world on how to buy without remorse, and live life as it should be lived. We will have no set itinerary, as that would work against our philosophy and our mission. We will probably set sail from Martha's Vineyard in Massachusetts, and there's no telling where we will go next. We will simply sail and land and land and sail, striking fear in the hearts of the sedate and thrilling women everywhere. It is hoped that we will circumnavigate the globe within three years.

We are well qualified for such an rigorous task. Mimi is adept at parasailing and deep-sea diving and has inspired masses to abandon work in the middle of the day and go swimming. Of the six employers she has had in the last three years, all six have said, "She's a real pistol. I'm inspired." She received her first class captain's license in 2009 and has undertaken over thirty month-long journeys with other people's boats. Lisa can knock a thimble off a rattlesnake's head at fifty yards with a bow and arrow. She has climbed to the top of Mount Kilimanjaro twice, and was awarded citations for bravery by the Parks Association. Her niece says, "Lisa is an adventure seeker and an inspiration. I hope I can be like her when I grow up." Both Lisa and Mimi are members of I'm Going to Have a Good Time Club, an association whose members have enjoyed themselves in unlikely places ranging from high school dances to sociology doctoral programs.

There is both the need and the opportunity to have some women living their best life in these trying times. Society needs this, the balance of the world needs it, and we need it. We can have a good enough time for every person on Earth; you can help us to do so. Two women in a sailboat whooping it up can only help the state of the world, and we ask you to fund this project. It's a worthy cause.

Edited Version by Lisa

Everyone craves adventure. Executives tucked away in offices, professors stranded in ivy covered buildings, doc- ~~tors~~ overworked in emergency rooms, parents exhausted from car-pooling; all ~~of them~~ dream of mountain climb- ing or deep-sea diving or traveling through Amazon jun- gles. Everyone craves adventure, but most people find it vicariously. People want images of adventurous people to inspire them, and consider how many of those executives, professors, doctors, and parents are women. There is a lack of daring images of women, and people are willing to pay for them when they can find them. Consider the success of Thelma & Louise, a film about women finding adventure on the open road. Women did not go on shooting sprees, but they flocked in droves to see the movie; it was one of the seven most popular films of 1991. Yet it was the only reckless kick-butt female adventure film made over the next two years. Consider the public's interest in the antics of supermodels: "What are they doing now? What will they do next? Where are they now?" The supermodels traipse over Europe masking money, breaking hearts, and painting ~~the~~ towns red, and people hang on their every bad-girl

unnecessary pronoun

linked for increase demand for such

italicize film title

move. In "Absolutely Fabulous," the cult hit of British televi-

sion, a couple of women tear up London, leaving chaos

and nail polish in their wake. How ~~to~~ address this need?

We propose to buy a boat and take a free-wheeling ocean

going tour.

We propose to buy a sturdy ocean going sail boat and

adventure across the open seas. We will go from island to con-

tinent to island, taking risks and having adventures. We will

swim in the jewel-like waters if the Mediterranean and

scale the cliffs of Dover. What are the benefits? We will ~~be~~

sky-diving in Venezuela and ~~then we will sail off to Saint~~

~~Thomas.~~ A young boy will say, "Wow. The thought of that

makes me so happy I will not throw this bowl of mashed

peas on the floor but will instead wait for my mother to

take it from my high chair." We will ~~be~~ swimming in the

Aegean Sea and a politician in her office will pick up her

pen and say, "Gosh, the idea of ~~them~~ swimming makes

me so thrilled I will sign this treaty ending all war every-

where." We will storm into a meeting in Portugal and

everyone will talk about it for days, instead of harping on

the drab details of some actor's divorce, thus sparing both

the public and the actor. Aside from these benefits to the

public, we will be having a wonderful time, and in doing

so, will provide the world ~~of women~~ with role models, with

an idea of how to live life on the edge and to the fullest.

We will accomplish this plan with a grant of ~obvious~
$5,000,000. First we will buy the boat, and ~some necessary~
luggage, rations, and navigating charts. The money that
remains after this will be used as spending money so we
can instruct the world on how to buy without remorse, and
live life as it should be lived. We will have no set itiner-
ary, as that would work against our philosophy and our
mission. We will probably set sail from Martha's Vineyard
in Massachusetts, and there's no telling where we will go
~make point~ next. We will simply sail and land and land and sail, strik-
~clear, not~
~just women,~ ing fear in the hearts of the sedate and thrilling ~~women~~ people
~people~ everywhere. ~~It is hoped that we will circumnavigate the~~
~~globe within three years.~~

We are well qualified for such a rigorous task. Mimi is
adept at parasailing and deep-sea diving and has inspired
masses to abandon work in the middle of the day and
~redundant,~ go swimming. Of the six employers she has had in the
~unnecessary~ last three years, all ~six~ have said, "She's a real pistol; I'm
inspired." She received her first class captain's license in
2009 and has undertaken over thirty month-long journeys
with other people's boats. Lisa can knock a thimble off a
rattlesnake's head at fifty yards with a bow and arrow. She
has climbed to the top of Mount Kilimanjaro twice, and
~be~ was awarded citations for bravery by the Parks Associa-
~specific~ tion. Her niece, Dana, says, "Lisa is an adventure seeker and an
inspiration. I hope I can be like her when I grow up."
Both Lisa and Mimi are members of I'm Going to Have
a Good Time Club, an association whose members

have enjoyed themselves in unlikely places ranging from
high school dances to sociology doctoral programs.

There is both the need and the opportunity to have
some women living their best life in these trying times.

repeat for emphasis

Society needs ~~this~~ it the balance of the world needs it, and
we need it. We can have a good enough time for every
person on earth and you can help us to do so. Two women in
a sailboat whooping it up can only help the state of the
world, and we ask you to fund this project. It's a worthy
cause.

Step 5: Put It All Together

Your proposal should be as professional as possible, so double-
check for typos, grammar, and spelling mistakes. The language
should be clear and convincing while conveying your enthusiasm for
the project at hand.

The title page of your proposal should indicate to the recipients
what they are to expect, and from whom. You should also include
information on how the recipients can get in touch with you, though
that same information should be included in your cover letter; see
Chapter 8 on professional letters.

Keys to the success of a proposal are much like those of a business
letter: brevity and knowledge of your audience. The cover letter for a
proposal should be no longer than one page, and it should include a
brief description of the project and the amount of money requested.
Also mention any significant prior contact with the funding source,
if relevant, and why you chose to approach this particular individual
or organization.

Sailing Sisters

A Proposal for a Round-the-World Voyage

Submitted by Lisa Smith and Mimi Smith

Everyone craves adventure. Executives tucked away in offices, professors stranded in ivy-covered buildings, doctors overworked in emergency rooms, parents exhausted from car-pooling: all dream of mountain-climbing or deep-sea diving or traveling through Amazon jungles. Everyone craves adventure, but most people find it vicariously. Consider the demand this creates for images of adventure to inspire them. Then consider how many of those executives, professors, doctors, and parents are women. There is a lack of daring images of women, and people are willing to pay for them when they can find them. Consider the success of *Thelma and Louise,* a film about women finding adventure on the open road. Women did not go on shooting sprees, but they flocked in droves to see the movie; it was one of the seven most popular films of 1991. Yet it was the only reckless kick-butt female adventure film made over the next two years. Consider the public's interest in the antics of supermodels: "What are they doing now? What will they do next? Where are they now?" The supermodels traipse over Europe making money, breaking hearts, and painting towns red, and people hang on their every bad-girl move. In "Absolutely Fabulous," the cult hit of British television, a pair of women tear up London, leaving chaos and nail polish in their wake. How can we address these needs? We propose to buy a boat and take a freewheeling oceangoing tour.

We propose to buy an oceangoing sailboat and adventure across the open seas. We will sail from island to continent to island, taking risks and having adventures. We will swim in the jewel-like waters of the Mediterranean and scale the cliffs of Dover. What are the benefits to the rest of the world? We will sky-dive in Venezuela, and a young boy will say, "Wow. The thought of that makes me so happy I will not throw this bowl of mashed peas on the floor but will instead wait for my mother to take it from my high chair." We will swim in the Aegean Sea and a politician in her office will pick up her pen and say, "Gosh, the idea of those two women swimming makes me so thrilled I will sign this treaty ending all war everywhere." We will storm into a meeting in Portugal and everyone will talk about the spectacle for days, instead of harping on the drab details of some actor's divorce, thus sparing both the public and the actor. Aside from these benefits to the public, we will have a wonderful time, and in doing so, will provide the world with role models, with an idea of how to live life on the edge and to the fullest.

We will accomplish this plan with a grant of $5,000,000. First we will buy the boat, luggage, rations, and navigating charts. The money that remains after this will be used as spending money so we can instruct the world on how to buy without remorse, and live life as it should be lived. We will have no set itinerary, as that would work against our philosophy and our mission. We will probably set sail from Martha's Vineyard in Massachusetts, and there's no telling where we will go next. We will simply sail and land, and land and sail, striking fear in the hearts of the sedate, and thrilling people everywhere.

We are well qualified for such a rigorous task. Mimi is adept at parasailing and deep-sea diving and has inspired masses to abandon work in the middle of the day and go swimming. Of the six employers she has had in the last three years, all have said, "She's a real pistol. I'm inspired." She received her first-class captain's license in 2009 and has undertaken over thirty month-long journeys with other people's boats. Lisa can knock a thimble off a rattlesnake's head at fifty yards with a bow and arrow. She has climbed to the top of Mount Kilimanjaro twice, and was awarded citations for bravery by the Parks Association. Her niece Dana says, "Lisa is an adventure seeker and an inspiration. I hope I can be like her when I grow up." Both Lisa and Mimi are members of I'm Going to Have a Good Time Club, an association whose members have enjoyed themselves in unlikely places ranging from high school dances to sociology doctoral programs.

There is both the need and the opportunity to have some women living their best life in these trying times. Society needs it, the balance of the world needs it, and we need it. We can have a good enough time for every person on earth, and you can help us do so. Two women in a sailboat whooping it up can only help the state of the world, and we ask you to fund this project. It's a worthy cause.

Step 6: Submit Your Proposal

Don't go overboard with your presentation; just make sure what you submit is neat and professional.

Common Project Proposal Pitfalls

Insufficient Evidence

When you write a project proposal, you must sell your idea, and as with all selling, the buyer is constantly wary of being taken advantage of. Give buyers, or readers, sufficient evidence; your enthusiasm must be backed up with facts.

No Visuals

Charts, graphs, and photographs contribute to a proposal's professional look, and break up the text to make it more interesting. Charts are also a great way to present hard data and statistics, which can help your case and convince your audience more readily.

Lack of Professionalism

If you do not appear entirely capable and organized, your audience is unlikely to trust you. Remember, you are asking readers to give you either money or control of some project, all of which makes recipients understandably nervous. It is your job to convince them of your reliability and capability.

Wrong Audience

Know your audience. If you are trying to sell a book about your experiences in the wilderness, don't send your proposal to a crossword puzzle publisher. This affects the way you write the proposal as well. Are you trying to convince an arts commissioner? Then your proposal should focus on that aspect of your work.

Lack of Enthusiasm

If you truly believe your idea is exciting, make sure your enthusiasm is conveyed. Most businesses receive hundreds of proposals, yours should stand out.

Format and Style for Project Proposals

Always Provide a Title Page

This should include to whom the proposal is being submitted, and your name, address, and where you can be reached. If it is a group project, it should list the name of the group or association proposing the project, as well as the name of one person to contact for questions and correspondence.

Footnote All References

The more documented evidence you have, the more creditable and impressive your proposal will be.

Charts, Graphs, and Illustrations

Be sure to assign any figures a number (e.g., Figure 1) so you can refer to them clearly in the text.

In Conclusion...

Like any type of writing, the best project proposals are clear, cogent, and backed up by research. As long as you take the time to organize and carefully edit your presentation, you should be able to put together a proposal that presents your ideas clearly and convinces a reader that you are the proper one for any job, project, or funding.

Recommended Reading

The following books are written especially for the business writer, and are invaluable for their information on structure, style, and presentation.

William Paxson, *The Business Writing Handbook*, Bantam Books, 1981.

William Paxson, *Principles of Style for the Business Writer*, Dodd, Mead & Company, 1985.

Key Takeaways

"Write like it matters, and it will."

—Libba Bray

That's it—you've made it through this book. If we can leave you with one small piece of wisdom, it's that you are a writer. Nearly everyone is a writer. Our everyday lives are filled with all different types of writing situations, from research papers and application essays to lab reports and project proposals, from work emails and memos to texts and comments posted on social media. Not all types of writing are high-stakes—that is, a promotion or funding or a passing grade is not always on the line. Still, it's essential to develop the skills necessary to convey your thoughts in a way that is clear, precise, organized, and thoughtful.

Remember, writing is not a task that only a talented few can truly do well. Writing is for everyone, and it can be done well by everyone. In most scenarios, writing is a formulaic process that can be broken down into a few straightforward steps. By following the guidelines laid out in this book, writing will become second nature. Writing tasks and assignments will become more doable and cause less panic and procrastination. With time, you may even find writing to be a relaxing exercise that can be empowering and therapeutic.

Our hope is that this book gives you the tools and confidence to go forth and conquer any writing task. When you approach writing in a practical way, you'll write well (and write smart) for life.

Appendix

Glossary

ACTIVE VOICE: Use of a verb so that the subject acts directly, as opposed to being acted upon passively

"I smacked him."

ADJECTIVE: A word that modifies a noun or pronoun

"*tall* tree" or "*silly* rabbit"

The words in italics are adjectives.

ADVERB: A word that modifies a verb, adjective, or other adverb

"She ran *quickly*."
"The *extremely* happy clam"

The words in italics are adverbs.

APOSTROPHE: A punctuation mark that shows ownership or forms a contraction

Ownership: *Pinky's* puppy

Contraction: *don't, wouldn't*

ARTICLE: A short word that functions as an adjective to indicate *which one. The* is the definite article; *a* and *an* are indefinite articles.

BIBLIOGRAPHY: A list of reference sources, usually books

CLAUSE: A group of words that contains a subject and a predicate

"Anyone who likes balloons should stay away from me."

The words in italics form a clause that is used here as a noun, and the subject of the sentence.

COLLABORATIVE WRITING: Writing produced by more than one person

COLON: A punctuation mark used to introduce a list or amplify the preceding thought

"These are the important things: food, shelter, and television."

COMMA: A punctuation mark used to separate words within a sentence

"She walked to the door, but she did not open it."

CONJUNCTION: A word that joins words, phrases, or clauses together

Examples: *and, but, because, yet*

COORDINATING CONJUNCTION: A conjunction that connects nouns to nouns, phrases to phrases, and clauses to clauses

Examples: *and, but, or, so*

CORRELATIVE CONJUNCTION: Also known as a seesaw conjunction, because it connects equal parts of a sentence together like a seesaw

Examples: *not only/but also, either/or, both/and*

DICTION: Word choice

ELLIPSIS: An omission, signaled by three dots. Used in quotations when part of the quote is left out. (He wrote "Man is always attempting...to prove himself.") An ellipsis can also be used to indicate that a thought is trailing off....

ENDNOTE: A note placed at the end of a chapter or a complete written work offering explanation, making a comment, referencing an author, etc.

ESSAY: A short piece of writing, usually analytical or interpretive, about a particular subject

FOOTNOTE: A note placed at the bottom of a page offering explanation, making a comment, referencing an author, etc.

INDEPENDENT CLAUSE: A clause that can stand by itself as a sentence

"*Rachel laughed at the landlord* and walked away."

Because the words in italics can stand alone as a sentence, they form an independent clause. A **dependent clause** is a group of words that has a subject and a verb but cannot stand alone as a sentence.

MODIFIER: A word or group of words that limits or qualifies another word or group of words in a sentence

"*red* apple"
"*Singing on the stage,* Kelly found her *true* calling."

The words in italics are modifiers, or modifying phrases.

NOUN: A word that represents a person, place, thing, or idea

"*Trees* are often pleasant."

The word in italics is a noun.

OUTLINE: An organizational plan for a piece of writing

PARAGRAPH: A subsection of a written work, typically beginning with an indentation on a new line, that focuses on a particular idea

PARENTHESES: Punctuation marks used to set off a qualifying or explanatory remark from the rest of the text

"Many people believe (more than they really should) that Santa Claus exists."

PHRASE: A group of words that does not contain a subject and verb but which functions as a conceptual unit within a sentence

"*Flying a kite* is torture for some."

In the preceding sentence, the words in italics are a noun phrase.

PRONOUN: A word that replaces a noun or noun phrase

"Grace said *she* is supposed to receive the million dollars."

The word in italics is a pronoun.

PROSE: Any writing that is not poetry

REDUNDANCY: The use of more words than is necessary to convey meaning

"She was *completely entirely* convinced."

The words in italics have the same meaning.

RESEARCH PAPER: An informative piece of writing about a particular subject that analyzes and evaluates a variety of outside sources

SEMICOLON: A punctuation mark used to separate independent clauses

"I went to the store; I hated everything there."

SENTENCE: A grammatically independent group of words, usually containing a subject and a predicate, that expresses a statement, command, request, exclamation, etc.

SUBJECT: The person, place, thing, or idea that the sentence is about (the subject performs the action or does the "being")

"*Joshua* won the lottery."

"Joshua" is the subject of the sentence.

TONE: The general style, character, or attitude of a piece of writing

Tone can be casual ("I'm going down to the corner store") or formal ("I am proceeding to the emporium at the edge of the avenue").

TOPIC SENTENCE: A sentence, generally at the beginning of a paragraph, that explains the main point of that paragraph

VERB: A word that expresses action or a state of being

"Keith *plays* the electric guitar."

The word in italics is a verb.

Commonly Asked Questions and Answers

Q: Is it okay to begin a sentence with *because?*

A: Sure, why not? For some reason "Don't start a sentence with because" is the one rule people remember from grammar classes, but there is no such rule. What you can't do is offer up a subordinate clause that begins with *because* and try to pass it off as a complete sentence. *Because it was raining* is not a complete sentence; it's a subordinate clause that needs to be attached to an independent clause. *Because it was raining, I took my umbrella* is fine. For more on sentence fragments, see Part 2.

Q: What about beginning a sentence with *and?*

A: Technically, you'll be writing a fragment. But if you want to do it on purpose, for emphasis, go right ahead. Sentences beginning with *and* are the stock in trade of copywriters, so we're all used to seeing them; the important thing is not to use them without good reason. And that's that.

Q: Is it okay to end a sentence with a preposition?

A: This is another one of those rules that people get overexcited about. (See?) Strict adherence to this rule can make for some mighty awkward and pompous-sounding sentences. So yes, if you are writing formally, recast the sentence so that a preposition does not fall at the end—but don't bother if doing so makes your sentence sound unnaturally stiff. (Winston Churchill (maybe): "This is the sort of English up with which I will not put.")

Q: Is it okay to say "OK"?

A: In formal writing, no. In informal speech or writing, sure, it's OK—and you can spell it OK, O.K., or okay.

Q: Is there a difference between *toward* and *towards*?

A: *Towards* is British; *toward* is American. Choose accordingly.

Q: I'm totally confused by *like* and *as*. Rescue me. Which do I use when?

A: Fasten your seat belt. Even accomplished writers get lost on *like* and *as*, partly because the use of *like* in speech has gone completely out of control. *Like* is a preposition, not a conjunction. Use *like* to make a comparison: *He looks like me. She acts like the president. Like Bob, Pinky wears red socks.* In all three sentences we are making comparisons: *he* to *me*, *she* to *president*, *Bob* to *Pinky*. *Like* should be followed only by a noun or a noun phrase.

It would be false, and pompous, to say: *He looks as I* (do). *As does Bob, Pinky wears red socks.* (Don't be afraid to use *like*.) *She acts as a president* could be correct, if you mean that she is acting in the capacity of a president, that she is actually doing whatever presidents do. But if you only mean to compare her to a president, stay with *like*. *Like* never functions as a conjunction, so if your comparison involves action, use *as* or *as if*: *Hershey's taste good, as chocolate bars should. Ralph ran as if his life depended on it.* In both cases, the *as* or *as if* is a conjunction that joins two clauses.

We're not done yet. Another trouble spot is the confusion between *like* and *such as*. Remember that *like* is for comparisons. *Such as* means *for example: For breakfast he cooked local specialties such as grits and red-eye gravy.* To say *like grits and red-eye gravy* would be to say that he didn't actually cook grits and red-eye gravy but some other food that was similar to grits and red-eye gravy. See the difference?

Q: **What is a split infinitive?**

A: Remember that an infinitive is the form of the verb that begins with *to*. *To play, to speak, to flee.* If you insert a word between the *to* and the rest of the infinitive, you are guilty of splitting the infinitive: to *happily* play, to *harshly* speak, to *quickly* flee. This is not a good idea, although it has become rampant even in good writing. If it doesn't lead to awkwardness and confusion, place your adverb on either side of the infinitive *to play* happily; *to speak* harshly; *to flee* quickly.

Q: **When should I say *good*, and when should I say *well*?**

A: Good question. Strictly speaking, *good* is an adjective and *well* is an adverb, although *well* can also be used as an adjective in certain circumstances, such as in describing health, satisfaction, or appearance (with the verbs *appear, be, become, remain, seem, feel, smell, look, sound,* and *taste*). If you have trouble remembering if you're doing well or good, just keep this in mind: Superman does good—you're doing well.

I did *well* on my test. (adverb)

I feel *well*. (adjective, describing health)

The doughnuts were *good*. (good is always an adjective)

Q: **What about *bad* and *badly*?**

A: *Bad* is an adjective, and *badly* is an adverb. Say *I felt bad when I woke up.* Not: *I felt badly when I woke up.* Follow the rules for *good* and *well*.

Q: Do you say *none is* or *none are?*

A: It depends. *None* is an indefinite pronoun usually treated as plural, unless you want to emphasize the individual parts, as in *not one single thing* or *no one single person.* When in doubt, go with the plural.

Q: Please explain that ugly *who/whom* thing.

A: Easy question. *Who* is the subject of a verb. *Whom* is never the subject of a verb. If you are confused, try to see whether you would use *she* or *her* in place of the *who* or *whom.* If *she* fits, use *who.* If *her* fits, use *whom. Who* is a subject pronoun; *whom* is an object pronoun.

    The girl asked who had called. (*she* had called or *her* had called? *She* had called, so use *who. Who* is the subject of *had called.*)

    The girl asked whom she should call. (should call *she* or should call *her*? Should call *her*, so use *whom. Whom* is the object of *should call.*)

In speech you can get away with using *who* for questions: *Whom did you call?* is correct, but no one is going to murder you for asking *Who did you call*? In writing, however, use *whom* when it's appropriate.

Q: Is there a rule about *shall* and *will?*

A: You bet. Use *shall* when there is implied intention: I *shall* return! Not: It *shall* be warm at the beach. You can also use *shall* for asking questions in the first person (*I* or *we*): *Shall* we dance? *Shall* I call you? Using *shall* in the second or third person implies a command or threat: You *shall* stay here until I say otherwise.

Q: Is there a rule about using *due to*?

A: Don't use it as a substitute for *because of* or as a prepositional phrase. An effect is *due to* a cause.

> **Correct:** His tardiness was *due to* traffic.
>
> **Not:** *Due to* traffic, he was tardy.

In the first sentence, *due to traffic* functions as an adjective; in the second sentence, *due to traffic* is a prepositional phrase. Is this giving you a headache? Follow this rule: don't begin a sentence with *due to*, and you will probably be safe.

Q: What about *hopefully?*

A: *Hopefully* is an adverb, meaning *in a hopeful manner.* We waited *hopefully* for the lottery numbers to be announced. It's incorrect to use *hopefully* when it doesn't modify a verb: *Hopefully, the nuclear threat is over.* Instead: *It is hoped* that the nuclear threat is over. Sound stilted? You could say *We hope the nuclear threat is over,* or some other variation.

Q: Is *percent* singular or plural?

A: It depends. ***The*** *percentage* is always singular: *The percentage* of young voters has risen. ***A*** *percentage* is singular if the object of the preposition is singular: *A percentage* of the work *is finished.* But *a percentage* is a plural if the object of the preposition is plural: *A percentage* of the reports *are finished.* The same rules apply when using *percent: Sixty percent* of the men *are wearing* hats. *Sixty percent* of the work force *is* absent.

Q: Can we go over *affect* and *effect* again?

A: Of course! Don't use *affect* as a noun unless you mean it in the psychological sense of *mood*. *Affect* as a verb means *to influence; effect* as a verb means *to bring about, to cause.* So *effect* and *affect* have two distinct meanings—which is partly what is confusing, because you could use either one correctly in the same sentence, although the sentence would then have two different meanings.

He *effected* changes in the corporate structure.

Her shoes *affected* her ability to run.

The weather *affected* my mood.

The weather *effected* tremendous damage along the shore.

His teaching had a poor *effect* on me.

The new drug *effected* his recovery. (brought about his recovery)

The new drug *affected* his recovery. (influenced his recovery—not clear whether the drug helped or hurt his recovery)

Q: When a two-part subject is connected by *or*, is it singular or plural?

A: It depends. Generally, treat the subject as singular, but if you have a singular and a plural subject linked by *or*, **make the verb agree with whichever is closer:** *The boys or Ralph is eating snails.* And: *Ralph or the boys are eating snails.* The second version sounds better, though both are correct.

Q. Wht abt txt spk?

A. It is always important to get your point across as succinctly as possible. When you're texting a friend, you should feel free to type any way that works for you (we use full words and punctuation ourselves). When you're writing for school or the SAT or ACT, it is important that you observe the rules of grammar and writing you have learned in this book. Not only will it make you look smarter, it will help you down the road when writing in college and later for work.

Common
Grammar
Mistakes

We did a highly scientific study to determine which grammar mistakes cause the most distress to the listener or reader. In other words, we asked around to find which grammar mistakes drive people crazy when someone else makes them. Here are the results:

To/Too; Your/You're; It's/Its

To is a preposition that indicates direction: I went *to* the dentist. *Too* means *also* or *excessive: She loved ice cream, but felt that some flavors were too extravagant, too. Your* and *its* are ownership pronouns; use them to indicate possession or ownership: *Your* slip is showing. *You're* and *it's* are contractions, shortened version of *your are* and *it is*. To say *You're slip is showing* would mean *You are slip is showing,* which would sound very silly.

Between You And I

This is quite common and quite irritating. Remember the trick for dealing with subject and object pronouns: do them one at a time. Between *you*. Correct. Between *I*. Incorrect. Since you would say *between me*, say *between you and me. Me* is the object of the preposition. The reason this error causes listeners such distress is that saying *I* instead of *me* is an attempt to sound stately or erudite.

Lie Versus Lay

This error drives some people crazy but isn't hard to explain. *Lie* never takes an object; *lie* means *to rest* or *recline*: I need to *lie* down. The books are *lying* on the floor. The principal parts for *lie* are: lie, lay, lying, lain. *Lay* always takes an object and means *to put down, to place*: He *laid* the books on the floor. He *will lay* himself on a bed of nails. Ask yourself, "Lay what?" In the sentences above, the answer would be *the book* and *himself*. If there is no answer, use *lie*. Strategy number two: if you can substitute *put*, use *lay*. Otherwise use *lie*. The principal parts for *lay* are: lay, laid, laying, laid.

Bring Or Take?

Use *bring* to indicate movement toward the speaker: *Bring* that book to me. Use *take* to indicate movement away from the speaker: *Take* that book with you when go. Not: I'll *bring* it with me when I go.

Their/There/They're

There can be an adverb, a noun, an adjective, or an expletive; *there* indicates location. *Their* is an ownership pronoun: *their pants* means *the pants that belong to them*. *They're* means *they are:* They're in their house, which is over there.

Infer Or Imply?

When you *infer* something, you are drawing a conclusion or making a deduction: I *infer* from your expression that you are upset. When you *imply* something, you hint—you don't state directly: By standing by the door, I *implied* that it was time for him to leave. You can draw an *inference* from someone else's *implication*, not vice versa.

Mispronunciations

This isn't exactly grammar. But some mispronunciations can make you sound unintelligent. Don't say heighth for height, nucular for nuclear, and strenth for strength, lenth for length, spaded for spayed, revelant for relevant. When in doubt, look up the pronunciation in the dictionary.

NOTES

NOTES

NOTES

NOTES